SANDHIYA'S HIGH-PROTEIN VEGAN MEALS

40-Min Vegan Cookbook for Weight Watchers

SANDHIYA IYYAPPAN

Table of Contents

Published by Sandhiya Iyyappan, 2025.

SANDHIYA'S HIGH-PROTEIN VEGAN MEALS

First edition. January 25, 2025.

Introduction

Welcome to a transformative journey of mindful, plant-based eating, where health and flavour converge to create meals that nourish the body, energize the spirit, and simplify modern living. This cookbook is a comprehensive guide to crafting high-protein, high-Fiber dishes that support weight management, improve digestion, and provide sustained energy—all while celebrating the vibrant and diverse possibilities of vegan cuisine.

Rooted in the timeless wisdom of my South Indian heritage, these recipes honour the traditions of preparing fresh, nutrient-dense meals using wholesome ingredients like legumes, vegetables, grains, and herbs. My ancestors lived long, healthy lives, fuelled by a simple yet effective approach to food. They prioritized balance, a deep connection to nature, and meals prepared from scratch—an ethos that remains profoundly relevant today.

Why High-Protein, High-Fiber Matters

In today's fast-paced world, maintaining a healthy lifestyle can often feel overwhelming. High-protein, high-Fiber meals are vital for building and repairing muscles, enhancing digestive health, and supporting effective weight management. Fiber promotes satiety while stabilizing blood sugar levels, and plant-based proteins provide a clean, sustainable source of energy without the heaviness of animal products. This cookbook is designed to empower you to enjoy these benefits effortlessly, without spending excessive time in the kitchen.

The 30-Minute Vegan Philosophy

1. High Protein, High Fiber: Each recipe is thoughtfully crafted with plant-based proteins like lentils, tofu, and quinoa, paired with Fiber-rich vegetables and whole grains to deliver a complete nutritional profile.

2. Quick and Easy: In recognition of today's demanding lifestyles, these recipes are designed to be prepared in 30 minutes or less, making them ideal for health-conscious individuals, including weight watchers.

3. Nutrient-Dense and Delicious: By using fresh, natural ingredients, these meals are both flavourful and nourishing. You'll find no processed ingredients here— only real, wholesome food designed to elevate your health.

4. Balanced and Sustainable: Inspired by the practices of my ancestors, these recipes embody the harmony between nourishment and simplicity, promoting a lifestyle that is both healthful and environmentally responsible.

A Celebration of Wholesome Living

This cookbook is more than a collection of recipes; it is an invitation to embrace the profound power of plant-based eating. Whether your goal is to manage your weight, boost your energy, or simply savour satisfying, nutrient-rich meals, these recipes offer something for everyone. Each dish is a celebration of health, vitality, and the joy of eating well.

Join me in rediscovering the elegance of simple, wholesome meals. With these high-protein, high-Fiber recipes, you will find that healthy eating can be both rewarding and perfectly attuned to the demands of contemporary life. Together, let's embark on this journey and make every meal a step toward your healthiest, happiest self.

Chapter1:Introduction to IndianVeganism: High-Protein, High-Fiber Meals in 30 Minutes

Indian cuisine has always been a cornerstone of plant-based eating, rich in tradition and packed with vibrant flavors. It's a culinary treasure trove that naturally embraces high-protein, high-fiber ingredients, making it the perfect fit for anyone seeking a nutritious and satisfying vegan lifestyle. From hearty dals to protein-rich legumes and whole grains, Indian food is a celebration of wholesome ingredients that nourish the body, mind, and spirit.

In today's fast-paced world, many of us are striving for meals that are not only nourishing but also quick and easy to prepare. Fortunately, Indian veganism offers just that: meals that are rich in plant-based proteins and fiber, ready in 30 minutes or less. These meals don't require hours in the kitchen, but they still pack a punch when it comes to flavor, nutrition, and satiety.

Why Choose High-Protein, High-Fiber Indian Vegan Meals?

Indian plant-based meals are a powerhouse of nutrition. With a strong emphasis on lentils, legumes, quinoa, tofu, and whole grains, they offer the right balance of protein to build and repair muscles and fiber to support healthy digestion and weight management. These nutrient-dense meals are designed to help you feel fuller for longer while providing a steady stream of energy throughout the day.

- High in Protein: Indian vegan meals often rely on lentils, chickpeas, tofu, and quinoa—excellent sources of plant-based protein that help with muscle recovery, repair, and maintaining a strong metabolism.
- High in Fiber: Fiber-rich foods like whole grains, legumes, vegetables, and seeds not only aid digestion but also help regulate blood sugar, lower cholesterol, and promote heart health. Fiber also plays a key role in weight management by keeping you full and satisfied for longer periods.

Additionally, Indian meals are brimming with antioxidants and anti-inflammatory compounds from herbs and spices like turmeric, cumin, ginger, and coriander. These spices not only enhance the flavor but also offer health benefits, such as boosting immunity and reducing inflammation in the body.

What to Expect from These High-Protein, High-Fiber Indian Vegan Recipes?

In this collection, you will find recipes that combine the richness of Indian flavors with the power of plant-based, nutrient-dense foods. Each dish is crafted to deliver a complete nutritional profile—packed with protein, fiber, and other essential vitamins and minerals. And the best part? All these meals can be prepared in 30 minutes or less! Here are a few examples of what you can expect:

- Chickpea and Spinach Curry: A classic, protein-packed curry made with chickpeas and spinach, perfect for a quick, flavorful meal.

- Tofu Tikka Masala: A plant-based version of this comfort food favorite, rich in protein and fiber, served with whole grains or roti.
- Quinoa Khichdi: A fiber-rich dish combining quinoa, lentils, and turmeric, ideal for a quick and satisfying meal.
- Sprout Salad: A refreshing, protein-packed salad made with mixed sprouts, vegetables, and a tangy dressing.
- Lentil Soup: A simple yet nourishing vegan soup that provides both protein and fiber, ideal for a cozy lunch or dinner.

These meals not only support a balanced, nutrient-rich diet but also respect the values of Indian cooking—where food is a reflection of health, vitality, and cultural heritage. Whether you are a seasoned vegan or just starting your plant-based journey, these high-protein, high-fiber recipes will ensure you get all the nutrition you need in a fraction of the time.

Key Benefits of These 30-Minute High-Protein, High-Fiber Indian Vegan Meals:

- Quick and Easy: Most recipes can be made in 30 minutes or less, perfect for busy individuals looking for wholesome meals without the hassle.
- Complete Plant-Based Protein: Enjoy the benefits of plantbased protein from legumes, tofu, quinoa, and other wholefood sources to build muscle and maintain energy.
- Fiber-Rich: Help maintain digestive health, reduce bloating, and promote heart health with fiber-rich meals.

- Packed with Nutrients: Enjoy meals loaded with essential vitamins, minerals, and antioxidants from fresh vegetables, legumes, and aromatic spices.
- Flavorful and Satisfying: Bold spices like cumin, garam masala, turmeric, and coriander provide layers of flavor that will keep you coming back for more.

Why Indian Veganism Works for a Busy, Health-Conscious Lifestyle

Indian vegan meals provide the perfect solution for anyone looking to nourish their body with the right balance of nutrients while saving time in the kitchen. You don't have to sacrifice flavor or nutrition just because you're in a rush. These recipes make it easier than ever to enjoy vibrant, high-protein, high-fiber meals that are not only satisfying but also aligned with a healthy, sustainable lifestyle.

Incorporating high-protein, high-fiber Indian vegan meals into your routine can help you feel energized, boost digestion, maintain a healthy weight, and support your overall well-being—all without complicated recipes or long cooking times.

Pantry Essentials for High-Protein, High-Fiber Recipes in 30 Minutes

A well-stocked pantry is the foundation for creating quick, healthy, and nutrient-dense meals. With the right ingredients on hand, you can whip up delicious Indian vegan meals packed with protein, fiber, and essential nutrients in under 30 minutes. Below is a curated list of pantry staples that will elevate your cooking and support your health goals.

1. <u>High-Protein Staples</u>

1.1 Lentils (Masoor, Toor, Moong)

- Why it's essential: Lentils are an excellent source of plantbased protein and fiber, aiding muscle repair, digestion, and providing long-lasting energy.
- How to use: Add to curries, soups, stews, salads, or make lentil-based veggie patties (tikkis).

1.2 Chickpeas (Garbanzo Beans)

- Why it's essential: Chickpeas are rich in protein and fiber, perfect for supporting muscle health, digestive function, and satiety.
- How to use: Use in curries, salads, hummus, or roast them for a crunchy snack.

1.3 Black Beans & Kidney Beans

- Why it's essential: These beans are loaded with protein, fiber, and essential minerals like iron.
- How to use: Add to soups, stews, salads, or make a hearty bean chili.

1.4 Tofu (Extra-Firm)

- Why it's essential: Tofu is a versatile source of plant protein, absorbing flavors from spices, making it a perfect addition to stir-fries, curries, and wraps.
- How to use: Pan-fry, bake, or toss into curries or salads for a protein-packed meal.

1.5 Quinoa

- Why it's essential: Quinoa is a complete protein, containing all nine essential amino acids, ideal for muscle growth and repair.

- How to use: Use as a base for salads, stir-fries, or as a rice substitute.

1.6 Peas (Frozen)

- Why it's essential: Frozen peas are rich in plant protein, fiber, and micronutrients, making them a convenient, nutritious addition to many dishes.
- How to use: Toss into salads, stews, soups, or stir-fries.

1.7 Sesame Seeds & Flaxseeds

- Why they're essential: These seeds provide protein, fiber, and omega-3 fatty acids, supporting heart health and digestive function.
- How to use: Sprinkle on salads, oatmeal, smoothies, or incorporate them into baked goods for an extra boost.

1.8 Peanut Butter (or Almond Butter)
- Why it's essential: Nut butters are rich in healthy fats and protein, adding richness to dishes.
- How to use: Blend into smoothies, stir-fries, baked goods, or make a peanut dressing for salads.

2. High-Fiber Staples

2.1 Whole Grains (Brown Rice, Barley, Millet, Farro)

- Why they're essential: Whole grains are fiber-rich and help with digestion, weight management, and stabilizing blood sugar levels.
- How to use: Serve as a base for curries, stews, salads, or grain bowls.

2.2 Oats (Rolled or Steel-Cut)

- Why it's essential: Oats are packed with soluble fiber, which helps reduce cholesterol and supports digestive health.
- How to use: Make oatmeal, add to smoothies, or use in baking recipes.

2.3 Sweet Potatoes & Regular Potatoes

- Why they're essential: These starchy vegetables are high in fiber, providing steady energy and rich in antioxidants.
- How to use: Roast, mash, or add to soups and stews.

2.4 Canned Tomatoes (or Tomato Puree)

- Why it's essential: Tomatoes are a good source of fiber and add rich, umami flavor to any dish.
- How to use: Add to curries, soups, stews, or as a base for sauces.

2.5 Frozen Vegetables (Spinach, Peas, Mixed Veggies)

- Why they're essential: Frozen vegetables retain nutrients and are quick to prepare, making them ideal for busy days.
- How to use: Add to soups, stir-fries, curries, or salads.

2.6 Avocados

- Why they're essential: Avocados are packed with fiber and healthy fats, promoting digestion and sustained energy levels.

- How to use: Add to salads, sandwiches, wraps, or as a creamy topping.

3. Spices and Flavor Enhancers

3.1 Turmeric

- Why it's essential: Turmeric contains curcumin, known for its anti-inflammatory properties, and also aids digestion.
- How to use: Add to curries, soups, stews, or smoothies for a golden touch.

3.2 Cumin & Cumin Powder

- Why it's essential: Cumin is a digestive aid and a core flavor in many Indian dishes.
- How to use: Add to dals, curries, vegetable dishes, and salads.

3.3 Garam Masala

- Why it's essential: This spice blend provides a rich, aromatic flavor to dishes with a balance of sweet, warm, and spicy notes.
- How to use: Sprinkle in curries, soups, rice dishes, and stirfries.

3.4 Coriander Powder (Ground) & Fresh Coriander

- Why it's essential: Coriander is known for its digestive benefits and adds a fresh, citrusy flavor to Indian meals.
- How to use: Add to curries, rice dishes, salads, and chutneys.

3.5 Chili Powder & Red Pepper Flakes

- Why they're essential: Chili powder and red pepper flakes provide heat, help boost metabolism, and enhance the flavors of dishes.
- How to use: Sprinkle on curries, soups, roasted vegetables, or salads for a spicy kick.

3.6 Asafoetida (Hing)

- Why it's essential: A small pinch of hing adds a savory, umami flavor and helps improve digestion.
- How to use: Add to the tempering for dals, vegetable curries, or stir-fries.

4.Fresh Ingredients for Flavor & Nutrients

4.1 Fresh Ginger & Garlic

- Why they're essential: Ginger and garlic are foundational to Indian cooking, offering depth of flavor and aiding digestion.
- How to use: Add to curries, soups, smoothies, or stir-fries for an aromatic boost.

4.2 Fresh Greens (Spinach, Kale, Methi, Mustard Greens)

- Why they're essential: Dark leafy greens are packed with fiber, antioxidants, vitamins, and minerals, supporting overall health.
- How to use: Add to dals, soups, or sautéed dishes for added nutrients.

4.3 Fresh Lemons

- Why they're essential: Lemons provide vitamin C and freshen up dishes with a zesty, tangy flavor.

- How to use: Squeeze over salads, curries, or grains for extra freshness.

<u>5. Other Essentials</u>
5.1 Coconut Milk (Canned or Carton)

- Why it's essential: Coconut milk adds creaminess to curries and soups, while providing healthy fats and fiber.
- How to use: Use in curries, soups, smoothies, or desserts for a rich texture.

5.2 Vegan Yogurt

- Why it's essential: Vegan yogurt is creamy and tangy, adding a probiotic boost to your meals.
- How to use: Use in curries, as a dip, or drizzle on chaat and salads.

5.3 Whole Wheat Flour (or Gluten-Free Flour)

- Why it's essential: Whole wheat flour is high in fiber and can be used to make roti, paratha, or as a binding agent for patties.
- How to use: Use for chapatis, parathas, or as a thickening agent in sauces.

5.4 Basmati Rice (White or Brown)

- Why it's essential: Basmati rice is a fragrant, fiber-rich option that pairs beautifully with curries and stews.
- How to use: Serve as a base for curries, vegetable pilaf, or grain bowls.

Quick Meal Ideas Using Pantry Staples

- Peas & Spinach Curry: Combine canned chickpeas, frozen spinach, tomatoes, and spices like cumin, turmeric, and garam masala for a quick, protein-packed curry.
- Lentil Soup: Cook lentils with canned tomatoes, garlic, and turmeric for a simple, fiber-rich soup.
- Tofu Stir-Fry: Stir-fry extra-firm tofu with frozen veggies, sesame seeds, and a soy-based dressing for a quick protein and fiber-filled dish.
- Quinoa Khichdi: Combine quinoa, moong dal, turmeric, and veggies for a quick and nourishing dish.
- Sprouted Bean Salad: Toss together sprouted chickpeas, quinoa, cucumbers, tomatoes, and a lemon dressing for a nutrient-dense, high-protein salad.

Chapter 2: High protein and High Fibre Breakfast Ideas

Breakfast Recipes 1:Spicy Protein Pancake

Prep Time: 10-15 mins Cooking Time: 15-20 mins

<u>Ingredients:</u>

- 1 cup store-bought mixed sprouts (legumes such as mung, peas, chickpeas, lentils, etc.)
- 1/2 cup rice
- 1-inch piece of ginger
- 1 bunch coriander
- 1 or 2 green chilies
- Salt (to taste)
- 1 tbsp coconut oil (for cooking)

<u>Method:</u> Day 1

1. Protein Pancake:
   - In a food processor, combine the mixed sprouts, rice, ginger, coriander, chilies, and salt. Grind into a smooth mixture.

- ◦ Heat a pan and add 1 tbsp of coconut oil. Pour the mixture into the pan, spreading it thinly like a pancake.
- ◦ Cook until crispy and golden on both sides.

Beetroot Chutney

Prep Time: 5 mins Cooking Time: 10 mins

<u>Ingredients:</u>

- 1 cup grated beetroot
- Equal amounts of roasted peanuts, almonds, cashews, and walnuts (about 2 tbsp each)
- 2 garlic pods
- 1 tsp grated ginger
- 1 or 2 green chilies
- 1 medium onion
- A handful of coriander
- 2 tbsp grated coconut
- 1 tbsp tamarind juice or lemon juice
- Salt (to taste)

- 1 tsp oil (for frying)

Method:

1. Heat 1 tsp oil in a pan and sauté the onion, garlic, ginger, chilies, and coriander until fragrant.
2. Add the grated beetroot and salt. Fry the mixture until the raw smell of the beetroot disappears. Sprinkle a little water to help soften the beetroot.
3. Add grated coconut and tamarind juice or lemon juice. Cook briefly.
4. Transfer the cooked mixture to a food processor and grind into a smooth chutney.

Serving:

- Serve the hot, spicy protein pancake with beetroot chutney on the side. Enjoy this healthy, protein-rich, and fiber-packed breakfast that keeps you full and energized!

Recipe 2: Vegan Protein Mashed Rice with Mung Beans

Prep Time: 10 mins Cooking Time: 15-20 mins

Ingredients:

- 1/2 cup Basmati rice
- 1/4 cup moong dal (yellow split mung beans)
- 1 tbsp coconut oil
- 1/2 tsp cumin seeds
- 1/2 tsp black pepper (adjust to taste)
- 1 tsp grated or finely chopped ginger
- 1 or 2 green chilies (slit; adjust to heat preference)
- 8-10 cashews
- 1/4 tsp hing (asafoetida; optional)
- 1 sprig curry leaves
- Salt (to taste)
- Water (for cooking rice and dal) <u>Method:</u>

1. Cook Rice and Moong Dal:
   - Wash the rice and moong dal under cold water until the water runs clear.
   - In a pressure cooker or pot, add the rice, dal, and 3 cups of water. Cook with 1/4 tsp turmeric powder until soft. (Pressure cook for 2-3 whistles on medium heat or simmer in a pot until creamy.) ∘ Set aside.
2. Tempering:
   - Heat coconut oil in a pan over medium heat. Add cumin seeds and let them splutter.
   - Add grated ginger, green chilies, and cashews. Sauté until the cashews turn golden brown.
   - Add curry leaves and hing. Cook for another minute.
3. Combine:

- Add the tempering to the cooked rice and dal mixture. Mix well and season with salt. Adjust consistency with water if needed.

4. Serve:

- Serve hot with coconut chutney. This dish is a wholesome meal, combining plant-based protein, fiber, and healthy fats.

<u>Tip:</u>

- For a richer taste, add a dollop of plant-based butter instead of coconut oil.

Coconut Chutney

Prep Time: 7 mins
<u>Ingredients:</u>

- 1 cup coconut (fresh or desiccated)
- 2 tbsp roasted peanuts
- 2 tbsp roasted almonds
- 2 tbsp roasted cashews

- 2 tbsp roasted walnuts
- 2 garlic cloves
- 2 green chilies (adjust to taste)
- Salt (to taste)
- 1 tbsp lemon juice

<u>Method:</u>

1. In a blender, add the coconut, roasted nuts, garlic, chilies, salt, and lemon juice.
2. Grind to a smooth or slightly chunky chutney as preferred.
3. Serve with protein mashed rice or any dish of your choice.

Recipe 3: Quinoa Savory Pancake

Prep Time: 10 mins Cooking Time: 15 mins Soaking Time: 4-6 hours Fermentation: Overnight <u>Ingredients:</u>

- 1 cup mixed quinoa
- 1 cup basmati rice

- 1/2 cup urad dal (split black gram)
- 2 cups water (for grinding)
- Salt (to taste)

For Chopped Vegetables:

- 1 tomato (finely chopped)
- 1 red onion (finely chopped)
- Fresh coriander (chopped)
- 1 jalapeño (finely chopped)
- 1 carrot (grated)
- 1 beetroot (grated)
- Salt (to taste)

For Garlic Masala:

- 1 tbsp chili powder
- 3 garlic cloves
- 1 tbsp garam masala
- Salt (to taste)
- 1 tbsp oil

For Cooking:

- Coconut oil (for frying)
- 1/4 cup shredded tofu <u>Method:</u>

1. Prepare the Batter:
    - Wash and rinse quinoa, basmati rice, and urad dal thoroughly.
    - Soak the mixture overnight. Grind the soaked grains with 2 cups of water until smooth.
    - Add salt, cover, and ferment for half a day.
2. Prepare Chopped Vegetables:
    - Mix chopped tomatoes, onion, coriander, jalapeño, carrot, beetroot, and salt in a bowl.
3. Prepare Garlic Masala:
    - Grind chili powder, garlic, garam masala, salt, and oil into a paste.
4. Cook Pancakes:
    - Heat a non-stick pan with coconut oil. Spread the fermented batter into a pancake shape.
    - Top with garlic masala paste, chopped veggies, and shredded tofu. Cook on both sides.
5. Serve:
    - Serve hot with coconut chutney.

Breakfast 4:Beetroot Waffles

Prep Time: 10 mins Cooking Time: 20 mins

Ingredients:

- 2 medium-sized beetroots, steamed and peeled
- 1 cup oats
- 1/2 cup roasted semolina (suji)
- 1 jalapeño, finely chopped
- 1 tsp cumin seeds
- Pinch of coriander powder and black pepper
- Handful of fresh coriander, chopped
- Small piece of ginger
- 1 grated carrot
- 1 small onion, finely chopped
- 100g tofu, grated
- Salt, to taste
- Water (as needed to adjust batter consistency)

Method:

1. Prepare the Ingredients:
    - Steam and peel the beetroots. Grate them or blend into a smooth puree.
    - Grate the tofu. Finely chop the onion, jalapeño, and coriander.
2. Roast the Oats and Semolina:
    - Roast the oats with a pinch of coriander powder, black pepper, and cumin seeds in a dry pan for a few minutes until fragrant. Cool and grind into a fine powder.
    - Mix the ground oats with roasted semolina.
3. Make the Beetroot Paste:
    - Blend steamed beetroot, cumin seeds, jalapeño, and ginger into a smooth paste.
4. Prepare the Batter:
    - In a mixing bowl, combine the oat-semolina mixture, beetroot paste, grated carrot, chopped onion, coriander, and grated tofu.
    - Season with salt and mix into a thick, smooth batter. Adjust with water if necessary.
5. Cook the Waffles:
    - Preheat a waffle maker and lightly grease it.
    - Pour the batter into the waffle maker and cook until golden brown and crispy.
6. Serve:
    - Serve warm with green chutney or dairy-free yogurt.

Green Chutney

<u>Ingredients:</u>

- A handful of fresh coriander, chopped
- 2 garlic cloves
- 1 jalapeño
- 1 tbsp lemon juice
- 2 tbsp roasted peanuts
- Salt, to taste

<u>Method:</u>

1. Add all ingredients to a blender.
2. Blend into a smooth paste, adding water as needed to adjust consistency.

Breakfast 5: Semolina Pancakes

Prep Time: 10 mins. Cooking Time: 20 mins

<u>Ingredients:</u>

- 1 cup semolina
- 1 cup vegan yogurt
- 1/2 cup roasted oats
- 2 cups water
- 1/4 tsp baking soda
- Grated vegetables (carrot, mashed peas, chopped onion)
- 1 tbsp curry leaves
- 1/4 tsp asafoetida (hing)
- 1 finely chopped jalapeño (optional)
- Handful of fresh coriander, chopped
- Salt, to taste
- Vegan ghee or coconut oil (for cooking)

<u>Method:</u>

1. Prepare the Batter:
   - Mix semolina, yogurt, roasted oats, water, and

baking soda. Let it rest for 1 hour. Adjust with water if thick.

2. Add Veggies and Seasoning:
   - Add grated vegetables and mashed peas.
   - In a small pan, heat oil, add curry leaves and hing, and pour it into the batter. Add jalapeño, coriander, and salt.
3. Cook the Pancakes:
   - Heat a pan with vegan ghee or coconut oil.
   - Pour batter, spread, and cook until golden on both sides.
4. Serve:
   - Serve warm with coconut chutney.

Coconut Chutney

Ingredients:

- 1 cup shredded coconut
- 2 shallots
- 1 jalapeño
- 1-inch piece of ginger
- 1/4 cup roasted almonds and walnuts
- Handful of fresh coriander
- Salt, to taste

Method:

1. Blend all ingredients into a smooth chutney, adding water if needed.
2. Serve with semolina pancakes.

Breakfast 6: Yellow Moong Dhall Pancake

Prep Time: 10 mins Cooking Time: 20 mins

<u>Ingredients:</u>

- 1 cup yellow moong dhall (soaked for 5 hours)
- Salt, to taste
- 1/2 tsp turmeric powder
- 1/2 tsp cumin seeds
- 1 tsp grated ginger
- 1 small grated carrot
- 1 small grated beetroot
- Some corn kernels (optional)
- 1 small onion, finely chopped
- 1-2 capsicums, sliced into rings (remove seeds)
- Fresh coriander, for garnish

<u>For the Tangy Tomato Chutney:</u>

- 3 ripe tomatoes
- Salt, to taste
- 1/2 tsp chili powder
- 1/2 tsp sugar
- 1 tbsp oil
- 1/2 tsp mustard seeds
- 2 cloves garlic, finely chopped Method:

1. Prepare the Moong Dhall Batter:
   - Soak 1 cup of yellow moong dhall for 5 hours. Drain the water and transfer the dhall to a food processor.
   - Grind the soaked moong dhall into a smooth paste. Adjust the consistency by adding a little water if needed.
   - Add salt, turmeric powder, cumin seeds, grated ginger, grated carrot, grated beetroot, corn kernels, and chopped onion into the batter. Mix everything well.

2. Cook the Pancakes:
    - Slice the capsicum into rings and remove all the seeds.
    - Heat a skillet or non-stick pan and place the capsicum rings in the pan.
    - Pour the moong dhall batter into the capsicum rings, filling them completely.
    - Cook the pancakes on medium heat until the edges turn golden and crispy. Then, flip and cook the other side until golden as well.

3. Prepare the Tangy Tomato Chutney:
    - In a food processor, blend 3 tomatoes, salt, chili powder, and sugar to make a smooth tomato puree.
    - Heat 1 tbsp oil in a pan, add mustard seeds, and let them crackle.
    - Add 2 finely chopped garlic cloves and sauté until golden.
    - Pour the tomato puree into the pan and cook until the oil separates from the chutney (about 5-7 minutes). Turn off the heat.

4. Serve:
    - Once the pancakes are cooked, serve them topped with raw onion slices, tomato chutney, and a sprinkle of fresh coriander.

Notes:

- For Extra Protein: Add a handful of chopped spinach or other greens to the batter for added nutrition.

- Chutney Tip: Adjust the sugar and chili powder in the chutney according to your taste for a tangy or spicier flavor.

Yellow Moong Dal Pancakes with Tomato Chutney are not only nutritious and delicious but also offer numerous health benefits. This meal is:

- High in plant-based protein for muscle growth and repair.
- Rich in fiber to support digestion and weight management.
- Beneficial for heart health, bone strength, and skin health.
- Packed with vitamins, minerals, and antioxidants that boost immunity, fight inflammation, and promote overall wellness.

Breakfast 7: Bread Sandwich with Mint-Coriander Chutney

Prep Time: 10 mins Cooking Time: 20 mins

<u>Ingredients:</u>

For the Sandwich:

- 2 slices sourdough or multigrain bread
- 1 cup parboiled potato, mashed
- 1/2 grated carrot
- 2 tbsp cucumber, finely chopped
- 1 tbsp capsicum, finely chopped
- 2 tbsp tomatoes, finely chopped
- Salt and pepper, to taste
- 1 tbsp fresh coriander, chopped
- 1 jalapeño, finely chopped (optional for spice)
- 100g vegan cheddar cheese, sliced or grated

For the Garlic-Butter Spread:

- 2 tbsp vegan butter (softened)
- 1 garlic clove, finely chopped

- 1 tbsp fresh mint, chopped
- 1 tbsp fresh coriander, chopped
- Pinch of salt and pepper

For the Mint-Coriander Chutney:

- Handful of mint leaves
- Handful of coriander leaves
- 2-3 garlic cloves
- 2 tbsp roasted peanuts
- 2 tbsp roasted almonds
- 2 tbsp roasted walnuts
- Salt, to taste
- Juice of 1 lime

<u>Method:</u>

1. Prepare the Sandwich Filling:
     - In a mixing bowl, combine the mashed parboiled potato, grated carrot, chopped cucumber, capsicum, tomatoes, and fresh coriander.
     - Add salt and pepper to taste and mix everything well.
     - Stir in the chopped jalapeño for an extra spicy kick (optional).
2. Prepare the Garlic-Butter Spread:
     - In a small bowl, combine the softened vegan butter with finely chopped garlic, mint, and coriander, along with salt and pepper.
     - Mix well to form a fragrant, herbed butter.
3. Assemble the Sandwich:

- Take two slices of bread (sourdough or multigrain). Spread a generous amount of the garlic-mint butter on one side of each bread slice.
- Spread the vegetable filling mixture evenly on one slice of bread.
- Top the mixture with vegan cheddar cheese (grated or sliced).
- Place the second slice of bread on top, buttered side facing outward.

4. Toast the Sandwich:
   - Heat a sandwich maker or griddle pan.
   - Place the sandwich inside the sandwich maker, pressing it lightly, or grill it in a pan, turning it once, until both sides are golden brown and crispy.
   - If using a griddle pan, you can apply extra butter on the outside of the bread for a crispier finish.

5. Prepare the Mint-Coriander Chutney:
   - In a food processor, combine the mint leaves, coriander leaves, garlic, roasted peanuts, almonds, walnuts, salt, and lime juice.
   - Grind everything until smooth, adding a little water if necessary to achieve the desired chutney consistency.

6. Serve:
   - Once the sandwich is toasted to perfection, cut it into halves or quarters.
   - Serve it hot with a side of mint-coriander chutney and tomato ketchup.

Breakfast 8: High-Protein Avocado on Toast with Beet Spread

Prep Time: 10 mins Cooking Time: 20 mins

<u>Ingredients for Beet Spread:</u>

- 1 medium beetroot, steamed and peeled
- 1/2 block silken tofu
- 1 garlic clove
- 2 tbsp vegan yogurt
- Salt, to taste

For the Toast:

- 2 slices sourdough bread, toasted
- 1 ripe avocado, sliced
- 1 tbsp sesame seeds (optional, for garnish)
- A drizzle of honey (optional) <u>Method:</u>

1. Prepare the Beet Spread:
   - In a blender or food processor, combine the steamed

beetroot, silken tofu, garlic clove, vegan yogurt, and a pinch of salt. Blend until smooth and creamy.

2. Toast the Sourdough:
    ◦ Toast the slices of sourdough bread until golden and crispy.

3. Assemble the Toast:
    ◦ Spread a generous layer of the beet spread on each slice of toasted sourdough. ◦ Top with sliced avocado.

4. Garnish and Serve:
    ◦ Sprinkle sesame seeds on top for added texture and flair.
    ◦ Drizzle with honey or maple syrup for a touch of sweetness (optional).

Enjoy this high-protein, nutrient-packed avocado toast with the earthy richness of beet spread.

Breakfast 9: High-Protein Beet and Tofu Cutlets

SANDHIYA'S HIGH-PROTEIN VEGAN MEALS

Prep Time: 10 mins Cooking Time: 20 mins
<u>Ingredients:</u>
For the Cutlets:

- 1 tin kidney beans, drained and rinsed
- 1/2 block silken tofu
- 1 beetroot, steamed and grated
- 2 green chilies, chopped
- 3 tbsp finely chopped onion
- 1 grated carrot
- Handful of fresh mint leaves and coriander, chopped

Spices:

- Salt, to taste
- 1/2 tsp red chili powder
- 1/4 tsp black pepper
- 1 tsp dried mango powder (amchur)
- 1 tsp coriander powder
- 1 tsp garam masala
- 1/2 tsp cumin powder (jeera)
- 1 tsp chaat masala (optional for extra tang)
- 2 tbsp roasted besan (chickpea flour)
- 1 slice whole wheat bread, ground into breadcrumbs
- 1 tbsp sesame seeds
- 2 tsp coconut oil or vegan ghee for roasting the

cutlets For the Vegan Mint Raita:

- 1 cup vegan yogurt (soy, coconut, or almond-based)
- A dash of water (to adjust consistency)

- Mint puree (blend fresh mint leaves with a little water)
- 1 tsp chaat masala
- Salt, to taste

<u>Method:</u>

1. Prepare the Cutlet Mixture:
    - In a large bowl, combine the kidney beans, silken tofu, grated beetroot, chopped green chilies, onion, and grated carrot.
    - Add the chopped mint and coriander leaves to the mixture.
    - Sprinkle in the spices: salt, red chili powder, black pepper, mango powder, coriander powder, garam masala, cumin powder, and chaat masala. Mix well.
    - Add the roasted besan (chickpea flour) and breadcrumbs to help bind the mixture together.
2. Shape the Cutlets:
    - Once the mixture is well combined, shape it into small, round or oval cutlets (tikkis).
    - Roll each cutlet in sesame seeds to coat them evenly on all sides.
3. Cook the Cutlets:
    - Heat coconut oil or vegan ghee in a non-stick pan over medium-low heat.
    - Place the cutlets in the pan and cook slowly on each side until golden brown and crispy (approximately 7-8 minutes per side). Keep the flame low to ensure the cutlets cook through without burning.

- Once both sides are lightly browned and crisp, remove the cutlets from the pan.

4. Prepare the Mint Raita:
   - In a bowl, whisk together the vegan yogurt and a dash of water to achieve your desired consistency.
   - Add the mint puree, chaat masala, and salt. Mix well until smooth and creamy.
   - Adjust seasoning if needed.

5. Serve:
   - Serve the hot, crispy cutlets with a side of fresh mint raita.

Notes:

- The cutlets can be refrigerated before cooking if you want to prepare them in advance. Let them rest for a bit before frying to hold their shape.
- For a variation, you can also add other vegetables like peas, corn, or spinach to the cutlet mixture.

High-Protein Beet and Tofu Cutlets are a powerhouse of nutrition, providing:

- High-quality protein for muscle building and recovery.
- Fiber to promote digestive health and maintain gut health.
- Antioxidants and anti-inflammatory properties to protect against oxidative stress and inflammation.
- Nutrients like vitamin C, vitamin E, and zinc for skin health, hair growth, and overall well-being.
- Satiety and blood sugar stabilization, aiding in weight management.

Breakfast 10: Pearl Millet High-Protein Soup

Prep Time: 5 mins Cooking Time: 10 mins

Ingredients:

- 1/2 cup bajra (pearl millet) flour
- 1/4 cup vegan yogurt (curd)
- 2 cups water (adjust for desired consistency)
- Salt, to taste
- 1 tbsp cumin seeds
- 1 tbsp cumin powder
- Fresh coriander leaves (for garnish)
- Mixed veggies of your choice (such as onion, carrot, bell peppers, peas, etc.)
- Chili powder (optional, adjust to taste)
- Lemon juice, to taste

Method:

1. Make the Millet-Yogurt Paste:

  - In a mixing bowl, combine the bajra (pearl millet) flour and vegan yogurt. Add a small amount of water

    to create a smooth paste. Stir until there are no lumps.

2. Cook the Soup:
    - In a pot, add the water and bring it to a gentle boil. Gradually stir in the millet-yogurt paste while continuously stirring to avoid lumps.
    - Add salt, cumin seeds, and chili powder. Keep stirring while cooking to ensure the mixture thickens evenly.
    - Let it cook for about 5-7 minutes on medium heat, allowing the soup to thicken to your desired consistency.

3. Add the Fresh Veggies:
    - Once the soup is cooked, turn off the heat. Stir in the fresh veggies like onion, carrot, bell peppers, and coriander leaves. The heat from the soup will lightly soften the veggies while keeping them fresh and crunchy. 4. Finish and Serve:
    - Squeeze in a bit of lemon juice for a tangy kick and stir in the cumin powder for extra flavor.
    - Garnish with fresh coriander leaves and serve hot.

Serving Suggestion: Enjoy this nutritious, high-protein soup as a light breakfast or a healthy meal any time of the day. It pairs well with a side of whole-grain bread or a light salad. Nutritional Highlights:

- Bajra flour (pearl millet) is an excellent source of plant-based protein, fiber, and essential minerals like iron and magnesium.

- Vegan yogurt adds creaminess and probiotics for digestive health.
- The fresh vegetables provide vitamins, antioxidants, and crunch, while the lemon juice adds a refreshing zing.
- Cumin seeds aid digestion and bring a warm, aromatic flavor to the soup.

This Pearl Millet High-Protein Soup is an easy, wholesome, and filling breakfast option that's not only nourishing but also packed with plant-based protein. Enjoy it as a healthy start to your day!

Lunch Recipes 1:One-Pot Green Rice with Tofu

Prep Time: 10 to 15 mins Cooking Time: 15 to 20 mins

<u>Ingredients:</u>

- Equal amounts of spinach, peas, beans, and broccoli
- 1 cup basmati rice
- ½ block tofu
- 1 cinnamon stick
- 2 cloves
- 1 star anise
- 2 cardamom pods
- 1 onion, chopped
- 1 green chili, slit
- 1 tsp ginger and garlic paste
- Salt, to taste
- Fresh mint and coriander (a handful each)

<u>Method:</u>

1. Heat some oil in a pan. Add the cinnamon stick, cloves, star anise, and cardamom pods. Sauté for a few seconds until fragrant.
2. Add the chopped onion, green chili, and ginger-garlic paste. Sauté until the onions turn translucent.
3. Add the spinach, peas, beans, and broccoli. Sauté the vegetables, but be careful not to overcook them.
4. Add the rice, salt, and 1½ cups of water (for every cup of rice). Stir in some fresh mint and coriander.
5. Allow the rice to cook for 10–15 minutes, or until the rice is cooked through and the water is absorbed.
6. Cut the tofu into cubes and season with salt, pepper, garam masala, a pinch of chili powder, and a squeeze of lemon juice. Mix well.
7. Heat oil, vegan ghee, or vegan butter in a pan.
8. Add the tofu to the pan and toss it on both sides until it becomes slightly crispy.
9. Once the tofu is crispy, mix it with the prepared green rice.
10. Serve hot.

Notes: Green Peas and Tofu Rice is a balanced, nutrient-dense meal that's high in protein, fiber, and healthy fats, making it perfect for supporting muscle health, digestion, and overall energy. It's a great option for those following a plant-based or vegan diet while aiming to maintain a healthy weight or build lean muscle.

Recipe 2: High Protein Vegan Biryani with Vegan Raita and Pickle

Prep Time: 10 to 15 mins Cooking Time: 15 to 20 mins

<u>Ingredients:</u>

For the Biryani:

- 1 cup basmati rice (or any long-grain rice)
- 1 cup tofu, cubed (pressed to remove excess water)
- 1 cup mixed sprouts (store-bought)
- ½ cup mixed vegetables (carrots, peas, green beans, potatoes, cauliflower, etc.)
- 1 large onion, thinly sliced
- 3 tomatoes, chopped
- ½ cup coconut milk (optional, for richness)
- 2 tbsp coconut oil or vegan butter
- 2 tbsp biryani masala powder (store-bought)
- 1 cinnamon stick
- 3 whole cloves
- 1–2 bay leaves
- 4–5 green cardamom pods
- 1 star anise
- 1 tbsp fennel seeds

- Salt, to taste
- Fresh coriander (cilantro) leaves, chopped (for garnish)
- Mint leaves, chopped (for garnish)

<u>Method:</u>

1. Cook the Tofu:
    - Heat 1 tablespoon of oil in a pan and sauté the cubed tofu with 1 tbsp biryani masala and turmeric powder until golden and slightly crispy on all sides. Set aside.
2. Cook the Vegetables:
    - In the same pan, add another tablespoon of oil. Add the cinnamon stick, cloves, bay leaves, star anise, fennel seeds, and cardamom pods. Sauté for a minute to release their flavors.
    - Add the sliced onions and cook until golden brown. Remove half of the onions for garnish.
    - Add the ginger-garlic paste and cook for 2 minutes, allowing the raw smell to disappear.
    - Add the chopped tomatoes, turmeric, biryani masala powder, and a pinch of salt. Cook for 5–7 minutes until the tomatoes soften and the spices become fragrant.
    - Add the mixed vegetables and store-bought mixed sprouts (legumes), stirring well. If needed, add a splash of water and cook the vegetables until tender.
    - Add the sautéed tofu to the pan and mix everything together. If using coconut milk, add it now along with some water, and cook for another 2–3 minutes until everything is well combined.

3. Steam (Dum Process):
    ◦ Cover the pot with a tight-fitting lid. You can also wrap the lid with a kitchen towel to trap the steam.
    ◦ Place the pot on low heat and cook for 15–20 minutes, allowing the flavors to meld together and the rice to fully cook.

4. Serve:
    ◦ Garnish the biryani with rose petals, reserved fried onions, fresh coriander, and mint leaves.
    ◦ Serve the High-Protein Vegan Biryani with a side of vegan raita, pickle, and papad for a complete meal.

Notes: High-Protein Vegan Biryani, Vegan Raita, and Pickle make a nutrient-packed, delicious, and well-balanced meal that supports muscle growth, boosts immunity, improves digestion, and aids in weight management. The high-protein content of the biryani, combined with the probiotic-rich raita and antioxidant-packed pickle, offers a comprehensive nutritional profile that promotes overall health and well-being.

For the Vegan Raita:

<u>Ingredients:</u>

- 1 raw onion, chopped
- 1 tomato, chopped
- 1 green chili, chopped
- Fresh coriander, chopped
- 1 shredded carrot
- Salt, to taste
- A pinch of sugar
- 2 tsp lemon juice
- Vegan coconut yogurt (or any plant-based yogurt)

<u>Method:</u>

1. In a bowl, combine all the chopped vegetables and herbs.
2. Add salt, sugar, lemon juice, and vegan coconut yogurt.
3. Mix everything well and serve alongside the biryani for a refreshing touch.

Lunch Recipe 3: Spicy Sour Falafel Curry with Piping Hot Rice and Healthy Crisps

Prep Time: 10 to 15 mins Cooking Time: 15 to 20 mins
<u>Ingredients:</u>
For the Curry:

- Store-bought falafels
- ½ can chickpeas (optional)
- 5 shallots, finely sliced
- 10–15 garlic cloves, minced
- 1 eggplant, chopped
- 1 jalapeño, chopped
- 1 potato, chopped
- 2 tbsp coriander powder
- ½ tbsp turmeric powder
- 1 tbsp chili powder
- 1 tbsp curry powder
- 2 tbsp tamarind puree
- ½ tin thin coconut milk (optional)
- Salt, to taste
- 1 tbsp sugar (optional, for balancing tanginess)

For the Rice:

- 1 cup rice
- 2 cups water

For Healthy Crisps:

- Store-bought vegan lentil crisps or homemade healthy crisps (optional, for serving)

<u>Method:</u>

1. Prepare the Falafel:
    - Steam the store-bought falafels for 5 minutes. Be careful not to overcook them, as they can become too soft.
2. Cook the Curry:
    - In a pan, heat some oil and add cumin seeds, mustard seeds, shallots, and garlic. Sauté until the shallots are softened and golden.
    - Add chopped tomatoes (2–3) and cook until they fully soften and turn mushy.
    - Once the tomatoes are cooked, add the coriander powder, turmeric powder, chili powder, and curry powder. Stir well to combine the spices.
    - Add the chopped eggplant and potato (cut into 4 pieces each). Stir everything together and cook for a few minutes.
    - Add salt to taste, tamarind puree, and one cup of water. Bring to a boil and simmer until the vegetables are tender.
    - Gently add the steamed falafels and ½ can of chickpeas (optional) into the curry. Let the falafels cook for another 5 minutes.

- If you like, add ½ tin of thin coconut milk to make the curry creamy. (This step is optional, but it adds richness.)
- For a spicy, tangy, and slightly sweet curry, add 1 tablespoon of sugar (optional). Taste the curry and adjust the seasonings as needed.

3. <u>Prepare the Rice:</u>
   - In a separate pot, rinse 1 cup of rice and add it to 2 cups of water.
   - Bring the water to a boil, then reduce the heat to low and cover the pot. Cook for 10–15 minutes or until the rice is fully cooked and fluffy.

4. <u>Serve:</u>
   - Serve the spicy falafel curry over the piping hot rice.
   - Optionally, add some healthy crisps on the side for an extra crunch.

Notes: Spicy Sour Falafel Curry with Piping Hot Rice and Healthy Crisps is a flavorful, satisfying, and nutrient-packed meal that offers a balanced combination of protein, fiber, healthy fats, and essential vitamins and minerals. It's perfect for anyone looking to enjoy a plant-based meal that supports muscle health, digestive well-being, boosts immunity, and aids in weight management. Whether you enjoy it as a fulfilling lunch or dinner, this meal is a great way to nourish your body while indulging in bold, delicious flavors.

Lunch 4: Steamed Rice with Kidney Beans Curry and Green Salad

Prep Time: 10 mins Cooking Time: 20 mins

<u>For the Steamed Rice:</u>

- 1 cup basmati or long-grain rice
- 2 cups water
- Pinch of salt (optional)

<u>For the Kidney Beans Curry:</u>

- 1 cup cooked kidney beans (or 1 can, drained and rinsed)
- 2 medium onions, finely chopped
- 2 medium tomatoes, pureed
- 1 tbsp ginger-garlic paste
- 2-3 tbsp oil
- 1 tsp cumin seeds
- 1 tsp turmeric powder
- 1 tsp chili powder
- 1 tsp garam masala
- 1 tsp coriander powder
- Salt to taste

- Fresh cilantro leaves for garnish

<u>For the Green Salad:</u>

- 1 cucumber, diced
- 1 carrot, grated
- 1 cup lettuce, chopped
- 1 tomato, diced
- Lemon juice
- Salt and pepper to taste

<u>Instructions</u>
<u>Steamed Rice:</u>

1. Rinse the rice under cold water until the water runs clear.
2. In a pot, bring 2 cups of water to a boil. Add the rice and a pinch of salt.
3. Cover, reduce heat to low, and let it simmer for 15-20 minutes until the rice is fully cooked and the water is absorbed.
4. Fluff with a fork and set aside.

<u>Kidney Beans Curry:</u>

1. Heat oil in a pan. Add cumin seeds and let them splutter.
2. Add the chopped onions and sauté until golden brown.
3. Stir in ginger-garlic paste and cook for 1-2 minutes.
4. Add tomato puree, turmeric, chili powder, coriander powder, and salt. Cook until the oil separates.
5. Add cooked kidney beans along with ½ cup of water. Simmer for 10 minutes.

6. Sprinkle garam masala and stir well. Adjust seasoning if needed.
7. Garnish with fresh cilantro leaves.

<u>Green Salad:</u>

1. Combine cucumber, carrot, lettuce, and tomato in a bowl.
2. Drizzle with lemon juice and season with salt and pepper.
3. Toss well and serve fresh.

<u>Nutritional Benefit:</u>

1. Balanced Nutrition: Combines carbs (rice), protein (kidney beans), and fiber/vitamins (salad) for a wholesome plate.
2. Heart Health: The fiber and antioxidants in kidney beans and vegetables support cardiovascular health.
3. Weight-Friendly: Low in fat and high in fiber, keeping you full longer without excessive calories.
4. Plant-Based Goodness: Vegan and rich in essential nutrients like protein, iron, and vitamin C.

Lunch 5: Chilli Garlic Fried Rice & Stir-Fry Veggies with Tofu

Prep Time: 10 mins Cooking Time: 20 mins

Ingredients for Chilli Garlic Fried Rice:

- 2 cups cooked basmati rice (preferably day-old rice)
- 2 tbsp sesame oil or vegetable oil
- 3 garlic cloves, minced
- 1 tbsp red chili paste or chili garlic paste (adjust to taste)
- 1 medium carrot, julienned
- 1 medium capsicum (bell pepper), thinly sliced
- 1/2 cup sliced mushrooms
- 2 tbsp soy sauce
- 1 tsp vinegar (optional)
- Salt to taste
- 2 tbsp spring onion greens (for garnish)

Ingredients for Stir-Fry Veggies with Tofu:

- 200g firm tofu, cut into cubes
- 1 tbsp cornstarch (for coating tofu)

- 2 tbsp oil (for frying tofu)
- 1 small zucchini, sliced
- 1 cup broccoli florets
- 1 medium red bell pepper, sliced
- 2 tbsp soy sauce
- 1 tbsp chili garlic sauce
- 1 tsp sesame oil
- 1/2 tsp sugar or maple syrup
- 1 tbsp toasted sesame seeds (for garnish)

Method:
For Chilli Garlic Fried Rice:

1. Heat oil in a large wok or pan over medium heat. Add minced garlic and sauté until fragrant.
2. Stir in the red chili paste and cook for 1 minute.
3. Add the julienned carrots, capsicum, and mushrooms. Stir-fry for 3-4 minutes until the vegetables are tender but crisp.
4. Add the cooked basmati rice, soy sauce, and vinegar (if using). Toss everything together to combine and coat the rice with the sauce.
5. Season with salt to taste and garnish with spring onion greens. Serve hot.

For Stir-Fry Veggies with Tofu:

1. Toss tofu cubes with cornstarch to coat them lightly. Heat oil in a pan and fry the tofu until golden and crispy. Remove and set aside.
2. In the same pan, add a little more oil if needed. Stir-fry zucchini, broccoli, and red bell pepper for 3-4 minutes.

3. In a small bowl, mix soy sauce, chili garlic sauce, sesame oil, and sugar or maple syrup. Pour this sauce over the veggies and stir to coat evenly.
4. Add the fried tofu back to the pan and toss gently.
5. Garnish with toasted sesame seeds and serve hot alongside the fried rice.

Lunch 6: Tofu Crumbled Rice

Prep Time: 10 mins Cooking Time: 20 mins

<u>Ingredients:</u>

- 2 cups cooked rice (preferably day-old rice)
- 200g firm tofu, crumbled
- 1 medium carrot, diced
- 1/2 cup diced mushrooms
- 1 medium bell pepper, diced
- 1 small onion, chopped
- 2 tbsp oil (sesame or vegetable oil)
- 1 tsp turmeric powder
- 1 tsp garam masala
- 1/2 tsp red chili powder
- 1/2 tsp cumin seeds
- Salt to taste
- Fresh coriander leaves for garnish
- Juice of 1/2 lemon

<u>Method:</u>

1. Heat oil in a large pan over medium heat. Add cumin seeds and let them splutter.
2. Add the chopped onion and sauté until translucent.
3. Add the diced carrot, mushrooms, and bell pepper. Cook for 3-4 minutes.
4. Stir in the crumbled tofu and mix well. Cook for 2 minutes.
5. Add turmeric powder, garam masala, red chili powder, and salt. Stir to combine and cook for another 2-3 minutes.
6. Add the cooked rice and toss to coat evenly with the spices and tofu. Cook for an additional 2 minutes to blend the flavors.
7. Garnish with fresh coriander leaves and a squeeze of lemon juice. Serve hot.

<u>Nutritional Highlights:</u>

- Tofu Crumbled Rice: Packed with plant-based protein from tofu and enriched with vitamins and minerals from fresh vegetables.

Enjoy these vibrant, protein-packed, and nutrient-dense Indian vegan meals! Let me know if you'd like additional tweaks or serving suggestions.

Lunch 7: Healthy Black Bean Burger

Prep Time: 15 mins Cooking Time: 20 mins

<u>Ingredients for Black Bean Patties:</u>

- 1 cup cooked black beans (or canned, drained and rinsed)
- 1/4 cup oats or oat flour
- 1/2 onion, finely chopped
- 1 garlic clove, minced
- 1 tsp paprika
- 1/2 tsp cumin powder
- 1/2 tsp chili powder
- Salt and pepper to taste
- 1 tbsp olive oil (for frying)

<u>Ingredients for Burger Assembly:</u>

- 4 whole-wheat burger buns, toasted
- Vegan mayo or hummus (as a spread)
- Lettuce leaves
- Tomato slices
- Beetroot slices

- Chipotle sauce (optional)

<u>Method:</u>
For the Black Bean Patties:

1. Mash the black beans in a bowl until slightly chunky.
2. Add oats, chopped onion, garlic, and spices (paprika, cumin, chili powder, salt, and pepper). Mix well to form a dough-like consistency.
3. Shape the mixture into 4 patties.
4. Heat olive oil in a pan over medium heat and cook the patties for 3-4 minutes on each side until crispy and golden.

For the Burger Assembly:

1. Spread vegan mayo or hummus on the toasted buns.
2. Layer with lettuce, a black bean patty, tomato slices, beetroot slices, and a drizzle of chipotle sauce.
3. Top with the remaining bun and serve immediately.

<u>Nutritional Highlights:</u>

- Black Beans: High in protein, fiber, and antioxidants, supporting muscle repair and gut health.
- Whole-Wheat Buns: Offer sustained energy with complex carbohydrates.
- Fresh Veggies: Add vitamins, minerals, and a refreshing crunch.

Enjoy these wholesome, nutritious lunch recipes designed to fuel your body and delight your taste buds!

Lunch 8: High-Protein Green Wraps with Onion Salad and Vegan Yogurt

Prep Time: 10 mins | Cooking Time: 20 mins
Ingredients:

- Wraps:
  - Homemade green wraps or store-bought spinach tortillas
  - Vegan butter or ghee for brushing
- Onion Salad:
  - 1 medium onion, thinly sliced
  - Handful of fresh coriander leaves, chopped
  - 1/2 tsp chili powder
  - Salt to taste
  - 1 tbsp lime juice
- Vegan Yogurt:
  - 1 cup vegan yogurt (soy, almond, or coconut-based)
  - Salt to taste

○   1/2 tsp chili powder
(optional) ○   1/2 tsp chaat
masala (optional) ○   Fresh
coriander leaves for garnish

<u>Method:</u>

1. Cook the Wraps:
   - Heat a skillet or tawa over medium heat. Cook the wraps on one side until golden spots appear.
   - For the second side, place the wrap directly over the flame for a few seconds to allow it to puff up. Quickly return it to the pan and gently press with a spatula or roti press to help it puff fully.
   - Remove the wrap from the pan and immediately spread a little vegan butter or ghee on the hot surface for extra flavor.
2. Prepare the Onion Salad:
   - In a mixing bowl, combine the thinly sliced onion, chopped coriander leaves, chili powder, salt, and lime juice.
   - Mix well and set aside to allow the flavors to blend.
3. Make the Vegan Yogurt:
   - Whisk the vegan yogurt in a small bowl until smooth.
   - Add salt to taste. Sprinkle with chili powder and chaat masala if desired.
   - Garnish with fresh coriander leaves.
4. Serving Suggestion:
   - Serve the wraps with the onion salad and vegan yogurt for a nutritious, balanced, and delicious meal. These wraps are rich in protein, fiber, and

antioxidants, making them an excellent option for a healthy lunch or dinner.

Lunch 9: Saffron Vegetable Biryani with Fried Nuts

Prep Time: 10 mins | Cooking Time: 20 mins

Ingredients:

- For the Rice:
    - 2 tbsp vegan ghee
    - 2 cups cooked basmati rice
    - A few strands of saffron, soaked in 2 tbsp warm milk
    - Fried onions, as desired
    - Salt to taste
    - Fresh coriander leaves for garnish
- Spices:
    - 1 small cinnamon stick
    - 5-8 peppercorns
    - 2 cloves

- ○ 3 cardamom pods
- ○ 1 tsp cumin seeds (jeera)
- For the Vegetables:
    - ○ 1/2 cup fried green beans
    - ○ 1/2 cup fried carrots
    - ○ 1 cup fried firm tofu or tempeh
    - ○ 1/2 cup fried capsicum (bell pepper)
    - ○ 1 cup fried diced potatoes
    - ○ 1 cup fried cauliflower florets
    - ○ 1/2 cup fried green peas
- For the Fried Nuts:
    - ○ 1 tbsp cashews
    - ○ 1 tbsp sliced almonds
    - ○ 1 tbsp raisins

Method:

1. Heat the Ghee:
    - ○ In a large, heavy pan, heat 2 tbsp of vegan ghee over medium heat.
2. Sauté the Spices:
    - ○ Add the cinnamon stick, peppercorns, cloves, cardamom pods, and cumin seeds. Sauté for 1-2 minutes until aromatic.
3. Add the Fried Vegetables:
    - ○ Mix in the fried green beans, carrots, tofu, capsicum, potatoes, cauliflower, and green peas. Let the vegetables absorb the spices for 2-3 minutes.
4. Combine the Rice:

- Add the cooked basmati rice and salt. Gently mix to combine, ensuring the rice grains remain intact.

5. Add the Saffron Milk:
   - Pour the saffron-infused milk over the rice and stir gently to distribute the color and fragrance.

6. Top with Fried Onions and Nuts:
   - Sprinkle fried onions, cashews, almonds, and raisins on top for texture and richness.

7. Cook on Low Flame:
   - Cover the pan and cook on low heat for 10 minutes to meld the flavors.

8. Garnish and Serve:
   - Garnish with fresh coriander leaves before serving.

<u>Serving Suggestion:</u>

Serve with Vegan Onion Salad and pickle for an authentic and flavorful meal. This biryani offers a blend of heart-healthy fats, antioxidants, and essential nutrients.

Lunch 10: High-Protein Tofu Wrap

Prep Time: 10 mins | Cooking Time: 20 mins

Ingredients:

- Tofu Kebabs:
    - 1/2 cup plant-based yogurt
    - 3 garlic cloves, grated
    - 1-inch fresh ginger, grated
    - 1 tsp garam masala
    - 1 tsp ground cumin
    - 2 tsp turmeric
    - 1 tbsp tandoori masala (store-bought)
    - Juice of 1 lemon
    - Salt and pepper, to taste
    - 600g extra-firm tofu, drained and cubed
    - 1 onion, cut into chunks
    - 1 colorful bell pepper, cut into chunks
    - Coconut oil for cooking
- Coriander Mint Dip:
    - 1 handful fresh coriander leaves

- ○ 1 handful fresh mint leaves
  - ○ 1/2 cup plant-based yogurt
  - ○ Juice of 1/2 lemon ○ Salt and pepper to taste •
- Green Salad:
  - ○ 1/2 onion, thinly sliced
  - ○ 1 tomato, diced
  - ○ 1 handful fresh coriander leaves
  - ○ A few handfuls of lettuce
  - ○ Juice of 1/2 lemon
  - ○ Salt and a pinch of chili powder to taste
- Wraps:
  - ○ Store-bought or homemade wraps

Method:

1. Create the Marinade:
   - ○ Combine yogurt, garlic, ginger, garam masala, cumin, turmeric, tandoori masala, lemon juice, salt, and pepper. Mix thoroughly.
2. Marinate the Tofu:
   - ○ Coat tofu, onion, and bell pepper with the marinade. Refrigerate for at least 2 hours, ideally overnight.
3. Make the Dip:
   - ○ Blend coriander, mint, yogurt, lemon juice, salt, and pepper. Set aside.
4. Prepare the Kebabs:
   - ○ Thread tofu, onion, and bell pepper onto skewers. Cook on a griddle pan with coconut oil until charred on all sides.
5. Prepare the Salad:

- Combine onion, tomato, coriander, lettuce, lemon juice, salt, and chili powder. Mix well.
6. Assemble the Wrap:
     - Spread dip on the wrap. Add kebabs and salad. Fold and roll tightly.

<u>Notes:</u>

- Use extra-firm tofu and press it to remove excess water.
- Soak wooden skewers in water before use to prevent burning.

Chapter 3: Dinner Recipe1: Mixed Beans Curry with Potato

Prep Time: 10 to 15 mins | Cooking Time: 15 to 20 mins

<u>Ingredients:</u>

- 1 onion, chopped
- 2–3 tomatoes, chopped
- 1 tsp ginger-garlic paste
- 1 tsp turmeric
- 1 tsp garam masala
- Salt to taste
- 1 cinnamon stick
- 1 clove
- 1 tsp fennel seeds
- 10–12 cashews, soaked in hot water for 30 minutes
- 1 tsp coriander powder
- 1 tsp chili powder (adjust to taste)
- 1 cup cooked mixed beans

- 1 potato, peeled and cubed
- 1 tsp sugar (optional) <u>Method:</u>

1. Prepare the Base:
   - Heat oil in a pan. Sauté cinnamon, clove, and fennel seeds until fragrant.
2. Blend the Onion Mixture:
   - Blend onion, ginger-garlic paste, and coriander leaves into a paste. Cook until raw smell disappears.
3. Add Tomatoes and Spices:
   - Blend tomatoes into a paste. Add to the pan along with turmeric, garam masala, coriander powder, and chili powder. Cook until fragrant.
4. Add Cashew Paste:
   - Blend soaked cashews with water and add to the curry base.
5. Combine Beans and Potato:
   - Add cooked beans and potatoes. Simmer for 7 minutes. Adjust seasoning with sugar if desired.
6. Serve:
   - Pair with steamed rice, roti, and a green salad for a complete meal.

Salad: Prep Time: 5 to 10 mins
<u>Ingredients:</u>

- 1 cucumber, chopped
- 1–2 tomatoes, chopped
- Fresh parsley and coriander, chopped
- 1 tbsp olive oil
- 1 tbsp lemon juice

- Salt to taste
- A little honey (optional)

<u>Method:</u>

1. Combine cucumber, tomatoes, parsley, and coriander in a bowl.
2. Add olive oil, lemon juice, salt, and honey if desired. Mix well.

Dinner 2: High Protein Sweet Potato Chaat with Sprouts Tikki

Prep Time: 5 mins

Cooking Time: 10 to 15 mins

A delicious and protein-packed chaat featuring sweet potatoes, mixed sprouts, and a burst of flavor from aromatic spices and tangy chutney. Perfect for a snack or light meal, this chaat is rich in nutrients, fiber, and healthy fats.

<u>Ingredients:</u>

For the Tikki:

- 1 cup mixed sprouts (boiled and strained)
- 2 medium sweet potatoes (boiled and mashed)
- 2 green chilies (finely chopped)
- 4-5 garlic cloves (finely chopped)
- 2 tbsp roasted gram flour (besan)
- 1 small onion (finely chopped)

Masalas:

- 1 tsp jeera powder (cumin powder)

- 1 tsp chaat masala
- 1/2 tsp salt (or to taste)
- 1/2 tsp red chili powder
- 1 tsp coriander powder
- 1/2 tsp ajwain (carom seeds)
- 1/2 tsp cumin seeds
- 1/2 tsp fennel seeds
- 1/2 tsp coriander seeds
- 1/4 tsp hing (asafoetida)

For the Chutney:

- Handful of fresh coriander leaves
- Handful of fresh mint leaves
- 2 tbsp tamarind paste
- 2 tbsp jaggery or coconut sugar (for sweetness)
- 1-2 jalapeños (for spice)
- 2 garlic cloves
- 1-inch piece of ginger
- Salt to taste

For Garnish:

- Vegan curd (for serving)
- 1 small onion (finely chopped)
- 1 tomato (diced)
- Pomegranate seeds (for a burst of sweetness)
- Chaat masala (for sprinkling)
- Sev (optional, for crunch)
- Fresh coriander leaves (for garnish)

Method:

1. Prepare the Tikki:
   - Boil the Sprouts: Boil the mixed sprouts in water until soft, then strain and set aside to cool slightly.
   - Blend the Sprouts: Add the boiled sprouts, chopped green chilies, and garlic to a blender or food processor. Pulse to form a coarse mixture (do not make it too smooth).
   - Combine with Sweet Potatoes: In a large mixing bowl, add the blended sprout mixture and the boiled, mashed sweet potatoes. Mix thoroughly.
   - Add Dry Ingredients: To the mixture, add the roasted gram flour, finely chopped onion, and all the masalas (jeera powder, chaat masala, red chili powder, coriander powder, ajwain, cumin seeds, fennel seeds, coriander seeds, and hing).
   - Form Tikkis: Mix the ingredients well and shape them into small round tikkis.
   - Cook the Tikkis:
     - Bake: Preheat the oven to 180°C (350°F) and bake the tikkis for 20 minutes, flipping halfway through for even crisping.
     - Air Fry: If using an air fryer, air fry the tikkis for about 10-12 minutes at 180°C (flip halfway through).
     - Shallow Fry: Heat a little oil in a pan and shallow fry the tikkis until golden and crispy on both sides.

2. Prepare the Chutney:
   - Blend the Ingredients: In a blender, combine fresh coriander, mint leaves, tamarind paste, jaggery (or coconut sugar), jalapeños, garlic, and ginger. Grind until smooth.

- Strain the Chutney: For a smoother chutney, filter it to remove any bits of herbs or spices. Set aside.

3. Assemble the Chaat:
   - Layer the Tikki: Place the baked or fried tikkis on a serving plate.
   - Top with Toppings:
     - Add a generous dollop of vegan curd over the tikkis.
     - Sprinkle finely chopped onions and tomatoes over the top.
     - Drizzle with the freshly prepared tamarind chutney.
     - Add a handful of pomegranate seeds for sweetness and crunch.
     - Sprinkle a pinch of chaat masala for an extra zing.
     - Garnish with fresh coriander leaves and a few crispy sev for crunch.

Serving Suggestion: Serve this High Protein Sweet Potato Chaat as a vibrant and delicious snack or a light meal. The combination of the savory tikkis, tangy chutney, and creamy vegan curd creates a perfect balance of flavors and textures.

Health Benefits: High Protein Sweet Potato Chaat with Sprouts Tikki is a nutrient-packed and flavorful dish that offers a wide array of health benefits. It supports digestive health, heart health, and weight management while providing a good balance of protein, fiber, and antioxidants. Perfect for a filling meal or snack, this dish is a great choice for those looking to fuel their bodies with healthy, wholesome ingredients. Whether you're vegan or simply looking for a delicious and nutritious option, this recipe will leave you satisfied and energized.

<u>Notes:</u>

- Sweet Potatoes: You can also use boiled or steamed sweet potatoes for added sweetness and a smooth texture in the tikkis.
- Customize the Toppings: Feel free to customize the toppings to your taste. Add cucumber, boiled potatoes, or even more pomegranate to enhance the flavors.
- Make it Spicy: Adjust the number of jalapeños in the chutney to suit your spice preference.

Dinner Recipe 3: High-Protein Dhall with Toasted Sourdough Bread and Green Salad with Avocado

Prep Time: 10 mins Cooking Time: 25 mins
<u>Ingredients:</u>
For the Dhall:

- 1 cup mixed lentils
- 3 cups water
- 1 medium tomato, finely chopped
- 1 medium onion, finely chopped
- 2 garlic cloves, minced
- 1-inch piece of ginger, grated
- 1 tsp turmeric powder
- 1 tsp cumin seeds
- 1/2 tsp red chili powder
- 1 tsp garam masala
- Salt to taste
- 1 tbsp coconut oil or vegan butter

- Fresh coriander leaves for garnish For the Toasted

  Sourdough Bread:

- 2 slices of sourdough bread
- 1 tbsp olive oil or vegan butter
- 1 garlic clove, halved (optional, for rubbing on bread)

For the Green Salad with Avocado:

- 2 cups mixed greens (spinach, kale, or arugula)
- 1 ripe avocado, sliced
- 1/2 cucumber, thinly sliced
- 1 medium tomato, diced
- 1 tbsp olive oil
- Juice of 1 lemon
- Salt and pepper to taste
- 1 tbsp sunflower seeds or pumpkin seeds (optional, for crunch)

<u>Method:</u>

1. Prepare the Dhall:
   - Rinse the mixed lentils thoroughly under running water and soak for 10 minutes.
   - In a large pot or pressure cooker, add the soaked lentils, water, turmeric powder, and salt. Cook until the lentils are soft and mushy (approximately 15-20 minutes on the stovetop or 3-4 whistles in a pressure cooker).

- In a separate pan, heat coconut oil or vegan butter over medium heat. Add cumin seeds and let them splutter.
- Add the chopped onions, garlic, and ginger. Sauté until golden brown.
- Stir in the chopped tomatoes and cook until soft.
- Add red chili powder, garam masala, and the cooked lentils. Stir well and let it simmer for 5 minutes. Adjust salt if necessary.
- Garnish with fresh coriander leaves before serving.

2. Toast the Sourdough Bread:
   - Brush the sourdough slices with olive oil or vegan butter on both sides.
   - Heat a skillet or grill pan over medium heat and toast the bread until golden brown on both sides.
   - For extra flavor, rub the toasted bread with a halved garlic clove while still warm.

3. Assemble the Green Salad with Avocado:
   - In a large bowl, combine mixed greens, sliced avocado, cucumber, and diced tomato.
   - Drizzle with olive oil and lemon juice. Season with salt and pepper.
   - Toss gently to coat the ingredients evenly. Sprinkle with sunflower or pumpkin seeds if desired.

Serving Suggestions:

Serve the hot, flavorful dhall with the toasted sourdough bread on the side. Pair it with the refreshing green salad for a complete, balanced meal.

Nutritional Highlights:

- Dhall: A rich source of plant-based protein and fiber, supporting muscle repair, digestion, and weight management.
- Sourdough Bread: A fermented, nutrient-dense carb option that pairs beautifully with the creamy dhall.
- Green Salad: Packed with healthy fats, vitamins, and antioxidants, promoting heart health and radiant skin.

Enjoy this wholesome and satisfying meal, perfect for lunch or dinner, that combines the best of comfort and nutrition in one plate!

Dinner 4: Green Dried Peas Masala with Raw Veggies on Top

Prep Time: 10 mins Cooking Time: 20 mins
<u>Ingredients:</u>
<u>For the Green Peas Masala:</u>

- 1 cup dried green peas (soaked overnight)
- 1 medium potato (optional, for thickening)
- 2 tbsp oil
- 1 large onion, finely chopped
- 1 tbsp ginger paste
- 2-3 tomatoes, chopped
- 1/2 tsp turmeric powder
- 1/2 tbsp coriander powder
- 1 tbsp chili powder
- 1/2 tsp fennel seed powder
- 1 tbsp garam masala
- 1/2 tbsp curry powder (optional)
- Fresh coriander leaves, chopped (for garnish)
- 1/2 tsp sugar (to balance the taste)
- Salt, to taste

- Water (for cooking peas and adjusting consistency)

For Raw Veggies (for garnish):

- 1 small onion, finely chopped
- 1 carrot, grated
- Fresh coriander leaves, chopped

Method:

1. Cook the Peas:
    - Soak the dried green peas overnight in water.
    - Drain and rinse the peas, then place them in a pot with approximately 4 cups of water for 1 cup of peas.
    - Add a little oil and cook the peas until tender. Optionally, add 1/2 potato while cooking to help thicken the mixture.
    - Once cooked, set aside.

1. Prepare the Masala:
    - In a pan, heat 2 tbsp of oil over medium heat.
    - Add the chopped onion and sauté until golden brown.
    - Add the ginger paste and cook until the raw smell disappears.
    - Stir in the chopped tomatoes and cook for about 3 minutes until soft.
    - Add the turmeric powder, coriander powder, chili powder, fennel seed powder, and garam masala. Stir well and cook for 5 minutes, adding a little water if needed to prevent burning.
2. Combine the Peas and Masala:

- ○ Add the cooked peas (along with some of the cooking water) to the masala mixture. Stir to combine.
  - ○ Adjust the consistency by adding more water if needed. The curry should have a soupy texture but not be fully mashed.
  - ○ Let it cook for 7 minutes, allowing the flavors to meld together.

3. Final Touches:
   - ○ Add 1/2 tbsp of curry powder, fresh coriander leaves, and 1/2 tsp of sugar to balance the flavor. (Optional: Add a slurry of roasted gram flour or cornflour to thicken the curry if desired.) ○ Stir well and cook for another minute. ○ Turn off the heat.

4. Serve:
   - ○ Transfer the green peas masala to a bowl.
   - ○ Garnish with raw chopped onion, grated carrot, and plenty of fresh coriander leaves. ○ Serve hot and enjoy!

Green Dried Peas Masala with Raw Veggies on Top is a nutritious and flavorful dish offering a wide range of health benefits. From plant-based protein and fiber to antioxidants, vitamins, and minerals, this meal supports your digestive health, heart health, weight management, and overall well-being. Whether you're looking to maintain a balanced diet, boost your energy, or improve your skin and digestion, this dish provides everything you need for a healthy, satisfying meal. Enjoy it as a wholesome lunch or dinner to nourish your body! <u>Notes:</u>

- The dish is best served with a side of warm flatbread or even as a soup on its own.
- You can adjust the spice levels by adding more or less chili powder, depending on your preference.
- The raw veggies on top add a fresh and crunchy contrast to the soft and flavorful peas masala.

Dinner 5: Haramara Kebabs

Prep Time: 10 mins Cooking Time: 20 mins

<u>Ingredients:</u>

- 1 bag of spinach (fresh)
- 1/2 cup peas (frozen or fresh)
- 1/2 block of tofu (pressed and crumbled)
- A handful of fresh coriander, chopped
- 1 jalapeño, finely chopped
- 1/2 tsp chaat masala
- 1/2 tsp chili powder
- 2 tbsp roasted gram flour (for binding)
- 1 boiled sweet potato (or regular potato), mashed
- 2 tbsp roasted gram flour (for binding)
- 1/2 tbsp garam masala
- Salt, to taste
- Oil, for shallow frying
- Whole cashews, for stuffing (optional)
- Lime wedges, for serving
- Your favorite sauces, for dipping (optional) <u>Method:</u>

1. Prepare the Spinach and Peas:
    ◦ Blanch the spinach: Boil a pot of water and add the spinach leaves. Blanch for 2-3 minutes, then immediately transfer the spinach into cold water to stop the cooking process. Drain and squeeze out the excess water from the spinach.
    ◦ Grind the paste: In a food processor, add the blanched spinach, 1/2 cup of peas, a handful of coriander, and 1 jalapeño. Grind everything into a smooth paste.
2. Prepare the Kebab Mixture:
    ◦ Transfer the spinach-pea paste into a large mixing bowl.
    ◦ Add 2 tbsp roasted gram flour into the paste as a binding agent.
    ◦ Add 1 mashed boiled sweet potato (or regular potato) into the paste for consistency.
    ◦ Grate the tofu and add it to the bowl.
    ◦ Add finely chopped garlic and ginger, 1/2 tsp chaat masala, 1/2 tbsp garam masala, and salt to taste.
    ◦ Mix everything thoroughly. Taste the mixture and adjust the seasoning if needed. If the mixture feels too runny, add more roasted gram flour to thicken it.
3. Shape the Kebabs:
    ◦ Heat a pan with a little oil for shallow frying.
    ◦ Take small portions of the kebab mixture and shape them into round or oval patties.
    ◦ Optionally, stuff each kebab with a whole cashew in the center for an extra crunch.
    ◦ If the mixture is too soft, add a bit more roasted gram flour to make it easier to shape.

4. Cook the Kebabs:
    ◦ Place the kebabs in the pan and shallow fry them on low to medium heat.
    ◦ Cook slowly to ensure the kebabs are cooked through properly. Flip them to cook both sides evenly until golden brown and crispy.
5. Serve:
    ◦ Once cooked, serve the kebabs with lime wedges and any sauces you prefer (like mint chutney or tomato sauce).

Haramara Kebabs are nutrient-dense, delicious, and healthy options for those looking to incorporate more plant-based meals into their diet. Packed with protein, fiber, vitamins, minerals, and antioxidants, these kebabs not only provide essential nutrients but also support various aspects of health, including heart health, digestion, blood sugar regulation, and muscle recovery. Notes:

- Binding Agent: If the mixture is too runny, always add a bit more roasted gram flour to adjust the texture.
- Optional Cashew: Adding a cashew in the center of each kebab gives a delightful surprise inside the crispy outer layer.
- Perfect with Sauces: Serve with tangy sauces like mint chutney or vegan yogurt-based dips for a complete meal.

Enjoy your Haramara Kebabs, packed with protein and flavor!

Dinner 6: Soya Kheema Masala (Vegan Minced Soy Protein)

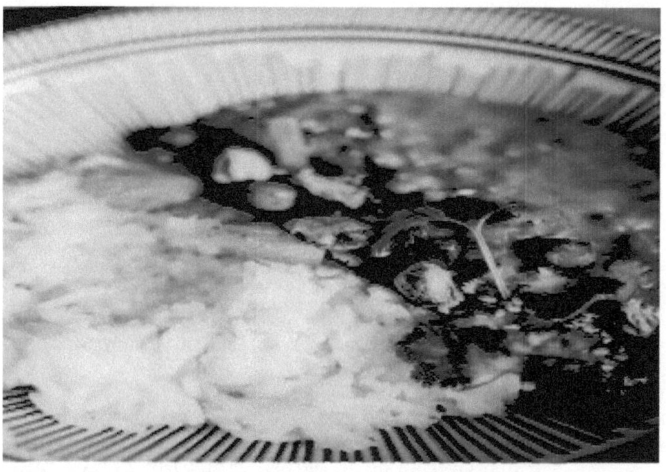

Prep Time: 10 mins Cooking Time: 20 mins
Ingredients:

- 1 cup soya granules or soya chunks
- 2 tbsp oil (coconut, olive, or vegetable oil)
- 1 large onion, finely chopped
- 2 tomatoes, finely chopped or pureed
- 1 tbsp ginger-garlic paste
- 1-2 green chilies, chopped (optional for spice)
- 1/2 cup peas (optional)
- 1/2 tsp turmeric powder
- 1 tsp coriander powder
- 1 tsp cumin powder
- 1 tsp fennel powder
- 1/2 tsp garam masala
- 1/2 tsp red chili powder
- Salt to taste
- Fresh coriander leaves, chopped (for garnish)
- 1 tbsp lemon juice (optional)
- 1 cup water (or as needed for consistency)

<u>Method:</u>

1. Prepare the Soya:
    ○ If using soya granules, soak them in warm water
      for about 10-15 minutes to rehydrate. Drain and
      squeeze out excess water.
    ○ If using soya chunks, boil them in water for 5-10
      minutes until softened. Drain, squeeze out the
      water, and finely chop or crumble them into small
      pieces. Set aside.

2. Cook the Kheema:
    ○ Heat oil in a large pan over medium heat. Add
      the chopped onion and sauté until golden brown.
    ○ Add the ginger-garlic paste and chopped green
      chilies (if using), and cook for another 2 minutes
      until the raw smell disappears.

3. Add Tomatoes and Spices:
    ○ Stir in the chopped or pureed tomatoes and cook
      for about 5-7 minutes until the tomatoes soften
      and the oil starts separating from the masala.
    ○ Add turmeric powder, coriander powder, cumin
      powder, red chili powder, fennel powder, and
      salt. Cook the masala for another 3-4 minutes,
      stirring occasionally, until the spices are well
      cooked.

4. Add Soya and Water:
    ○ Add the soaked and drained soya to the masala.
      Stir well to coat the soya in the spices.
    ○ Add 1 cup of water (or more for a thinner
      consistency). Stir well and let the mixture simmer
      for 10-15 minutes until the water evaporates and

the soya absorbs the flavors. You can add more water if you prefer a gravy-like consistency.

5. Add Peas and Garnish:
    - If using peas, add them to the kheema and cook for another 5 minutes until the peas are tender.
    - Stir in the garam masala and a squeeze of lemon juice for added freshness.
    - Taste and adjust seasoning as needed.

6. Serve:
    - Garnish the soya kheema with fresh coriander leaves and serve hot.

Soya Kheema Masala is a nutrient-dense, high-protein, and high-fiber dish that offers a wide range of health benefits, including:

- Support for muscle growth and repair.
- Rich in fiber for better digestion and weight management.
- Packed with essential vitamins and minerals like iron, calcium, and magnesium.
- Heart-healthy, low in saturated fat, and cholesterol-lowering.
- Hormonal balance support and immune system boosting.
- Antioxidant-rich, promoting healthy skin and hair.

Serving Suggestions:

- Serve Soya Kheema Masala with olive oil toasted sourdough bread or steamed rice.
- You can also use it as a filling for wraps, sandwiches, or tacos.

This dish is packed with plant-based protein from soya and is a hearty, flavorful, and nutritious option for lunch or dinner!

Dinner 7: Quinoa Khichadi with Green Salad

Prep Time: 10 mins Cooking Time: 20 mins

<u>Ingredients:</u>

For the Khichadi:

- 1 cup quinoa
- 1/4 cup split yellow moong dal (or your choice of dal)
- 3 1/2 cups water
- 1 vegetable stock cube
- 1 tbsp vegan ghee or coconut oil
- 1 tsp mustard seeds
- 1 tsp cumin seeds
- 1-inch piece of fresh ginger, grated
- 1 jalapeño, chopped (optional, for heat)
- 2 garlic cloves, finely chopped
- 6-7 curry leaves (optional)
- 1 tsp onion powder (or 1 small onion, chopped)

- 1 medium tomato, chopped
- 1/2 tsp turmeric powder
- 1 tbsp curry powder
- 1 small carrot, chopped
- 1/4 cup peas (fresh or frozen)
- 1/4 cup cauliflower florets
- 1/4 cup green beans, chopped
- Salt to taste
- Handful of fresh coriander, chopped (for garnish)

For the Salad:

- 1 small onion, thinly sliced
- 1 medium tomato, sliced
- 1 small beetroot, parboiled and sliced
- 1 small cucumber, sliced
- Juice of 1 lime
- Salt to taste

Method:

1. Cook the Quinoa and Dal:
   - In a large bowl, soak the quinoa and dal together for 15 minutes.
   - After 15 minutes, drain the quinoa and dal, and transfer them to a pressure cooker.
   - Add 3 1/2 cups of water and the vegetable stock cube to the cooker.
   - Cook on high for 4 minutes after the first whistle (you can also cook in a regular pot, just make sure the quinoa and dal are soft and fully cooked). Once done, set aside.

2. Prepare the Spices and Vegetables:
    - Heat the vegan ghee or coconut oil in a large pan over medium heat.
    - Add the mustard seeds and cumin seeds. Let them splutter.
    - Add the grated ginger, chopped garlic, and jalapeño. Sauté for 1-2 minutes.
    - Stir in the curry leaves (if using), onion powder (or chopped onion), and chopped tomato. Cook for about 3-4 minutes until the tomato softens.
    - Add the turmeric powder, curry powder, and salt. Stir to combine, letting the spices cook for another 2 minutes.
    - Add the chopped carrot, peas, cauliflower, and green beans. Let the vegetables cook for about 5 minutes, stirring occasionally, until they soften but still retain some crunch.
3. Combine the Quinoa, Dal, and Vegetables:
    - Add the cooked quinoa and dal mixture to the pan with the veggies and spices.
    - Stir well to combine, and let it cook together for about 10 minutes, allowing the flavors to meld.
    - Check the consistency; the khichadi should be slightly loose, not too thick, and not runny.
4. Final Touches:
    - Once cooked, remove from heat and stir in a handful of fresh coriander for garnish.
5. Prepare the Salad:
    - In a bowl, combine the sliced onion, tomato, parboiled beetroot, and cucumber.
    - Drizzle with lime juice and sprinkle with salt to taste. Toss well.

6. Serve:

   - Serve the warm quinoa khichadi alongside the refreshing green salad for a complete, nutritious meal.

Quinoa Khichadi with Green Salad is a powerhouse of nutrition, offering a wealth of health benefits, including:

- High in plant-based protein for muscle building and repair.
- Rich in fiber for improved digestion and weight management.
- Heart-healthy due to its high fiber content and beneficial minerals like magnesium and potassium.
- Packed with antioxidants to fight inflammation and promote overall cellular health.
- Supports bone health, digestion, and blood sugar regulation.
- Vegan and gluten-free, making it a versatile option for a wide range of dietary needs.

Enjoy! This quinoa khichadi is a comforting, protein-packed, and nutrient-dense dish, perfect for a light but filling meal. The blend of spices and fresh veggies gives it a vibrant flavor, while the quinoa makes it a great gluten-free option. The tangy green salad adds a refreshing contrast to the warmth of the khichadi.

Dinner 8: High-Protein Dal Makhani with Steamed Rice, Roti, and Green Salad

Prep Time: 10 mins Cooking Time: 20 mins

<u>Ingredients for Dal Makhani:</u>

- 1 cup black urad dal (split and skinned)
- 1/2 tsp turmeric powder
- 1 bay leaf
- 1 black cardamom
- 5 black peppercorns
- 1/2 tbsp cumin seeds
- Salt to taste
- Vegan butter (or oil for sautéing)
- 1 onion, finely chopped
- 2 tomatoes, chopped
- 2 tbsp ginger-garlic paste
- 1 tbsp chili powder
- 1/2 tsp garam masala

- 1 block tofu (200g), grated
- 10 soaked cashews
- 60g coconut milk (1/2 tin)
- Handful of fresh coriander leaves
- Vegan butter or oil (for cooking)
- 1 green chili (optional, chopped)

<u>Method for Dal Makhani:</u>

1. Cook the Urad Dal:
   - Rinse the black urad dal under running water. In a pressure cooker, add the dal, 1/2 tsp turmeric powder, and enough water to cover the dal.
   - Cook for 8 whistles (or until the dal is soft). Set aside.
2. Prepare the Onion Paste:
   - In a food processor, blend the chopped onion, ginger-garlic paste, and 1 green chili (optional). Set aside.
3. Prepare the Tomato Puree:
   - Blend the chopped tomatoes in a food processor to make a smooth puree. Set aside.
4. Make the Tofu-Cashew Mixture:
   - In a food processor, blend the grated tofu, soaked cashews, coconut milk, and a handful of coriander leaves until smooth and creamy. Set aside.
5. Cooking the Gravy:
   - Heat some vegan butter (or oil) in a pan. Add 1 bay leaf, black cardamom, black peppercorns, and cumin seeds. Let them sizzle for a few seconds.

- ○ Add the prepared onion paste and sauté until the onions turn golden brown and the raw smell disappears.
- ○ Add the tomato puree and cook for 5-7 minutes, stirring occasionally, until the oil begins to separate.
- ○ Add chili powder, garam masala, and salt to taste. Cook the spices for 2-3 minutes until fragrant.

6. Combine Dal and Tofu Mixture:
    - ○ Add the cooked urad dal to the pan and stir to combine.
    - ○ Slowly mix in the tofu-cashew-coconut milk mixture. Stir well to create a smooth, creamy consistency.
    - ○ Let the dal simmer on low heat for 5-10 minutes, allowing the flavors to meld together.

7. Final Touches:
    - ○ Check for seasoning and adjust salt if needed. Garnish with fresh coriander leaves and a drizzle of coconut cream if desired.

For Steamed Rice:
Ingredients:

- 1 cup basmati rice
- 2 cups water
- 1/2 tsp salt
- 1 bay leaf (optional)

Method:

1. Wash the basmati rice under running water until the water runs clear.
2. In a pot or rice cooker, add the rice, water, salt, and bay leaf.
3. Bring to a boil, then reduce the heat to low and cover the pot. Let the rice steam for 10-12 minutes, or until the water is absorbed and the rice is tender.

For Roti:
Ingredients:

- 2 cups whole wheat flour
- 1/2 tsp salt
- Water (as needed)
- Vegan butter or ghee (optional)

Method:

1. In a bowl, mix the whole wheat flour and salt. Gradually add water and knead to form a smooth, soft dough.
2. Divide the dough into small balls and roll them out into flat circles (use flour to prevent sticking).
3. Heat a tawa or griddle over medium-high heat. Cook each roti on both sides until brown spots appear. Optionally, brush with vegan butter or ghee for added flavor.

For Green Salad:
Ingredients:

- 1 cucumber, sliced
- 1 tomato, chopped
- 1/2 onion, thinly sliced
- Handful of fresh coriander or parsley

- 1 tbsp olive oil
- 1 tbsp lemon juice
- Salt and pepper to taste

<u>Method:</u>

1. In a bowl, combine the cucumber, tomato, and onion.
2. Drizzle with olive oil and lemon juice. Toss gently to combine.
3. Season with salt and pepper. Garnish with fresh coriander or parsley.

<u>Serving:</u>

- Serve the High-Protein Dal Makhani with steamed rice or roti on the side.
- Add the green salad for a fresh and nutritious balance.

Enjoy your wholesome, high-protein meal with the perfect balance of fiber, vitamins, and protein-rich ingredients!

High-Protein Dal Makhani with Steamed Rice, Roti, and Green Salad is a nutrient-packed, delicious meal that offers an array of health benefits:

- Supports muscle growth and repair with high plant-based protein.
- Promotes digestion and gut health with fiber.
- Aids in weight management by promoting satiety and reducing cravings.
- Rich in antioxidants and micronutrients to enhance overall health.
- Supports heart and bone health with essential vitamins and minerals.

- Boosts immune function with natural compounds in garlic, onion, and ginger.

This dish is a wholesome, satisfying, and complete meal for those looking to maintain a healthy lifestyle, improve their muscle mass, or simply enjoy a hearty, flavorful dish. Whether you are looking for a high-protein vegan meal or a comforting dish for a busy day, Dal Makhani with steamed rice, roti, and a green salad will nourish your body, support your health, and satisfy your taste buds.

Dinner 9: High-Protein Cauliflower and Chickpeas on Garlicky Whipped Tofu Sauce

Prep Time: 10 mins Cooking Time: 20 mins
<u>Ingredients:</u>
For the Cauliflower and Chickpea Topping:

- 1/2 cup cauliflower florets (washed)
- 1/2 cup cooked chickpeas
- 1 tbsp olive oil
- 1/2 tsp sweet paprika

- 1/2 tsp cumin powder
- 1/2 tsp turmeric powder
- Salt to taste
- 5 strands of saffron
- 2 tbsp warm water
- Fresh parsley, for garnish

For the Garlicky Whipped Tofu Sauce:

- 1 block silken tofu (drained)
- 1 garlic clove
- Juice of 1 lime
- Salt to taste

For Garnish:

- Chopped onion (optional)
- Chili powder (optional)
- Fresh coriander leaves
- Lemon juice (for a squeeze)

Method:

1. Prepare the Cauliflower and Chickpeas:
    - Preheat your oven to 200°C (400°F).
    - In a small bowl, soak the saffron strands in 2 tbsp of warm water, allowing them to release their color and aroma.
    - In a mixing bowl, combine the cauliflower florets and chickpeas. Add olive oil, sweet paprika, cumin, turmeric, and salt. Pour the saffron water over the mixture and toss well to coat.

- Spread the cauliflower and chickpeas in a single layer on a baking tray lined with parchment paper. Bake in the oven for 20-25 minutes, or until the cauliflower is tender and slightly crispy, and the chickpeas are crunchy. Stir halfway through to ensure even cooking.

2. Make the Garlicky Whipped Tofu Sauce:
   - While the cauliflower and chickpeas bake, prepare the tofu sauce. In a food processor or with a hand blender, blend the drained silken tofu, 1 garlic clove, lime juice, and salt until smooth and creamy. Adjust

   the seasoning to taste.

3. Assemble the Dish:
   - Pour the creamy garlicky tofu sauce into the base of your serving bowl, spreading it evenly.
   - Once the cauliflower and chickpeas are baked to perfection, top the sauce with the mixture.

4. Garnish and Serve:
   - Garnish with chopped onion (if desired), a sprinkle of chili powder, fresh coriander leaves, and a squeeze of lemon juice for a burst of freshness. ◦ Serve immediately and enjoy!

Serving Suggestion: This dish pairs beautifully with warm pita bread or steamed quinoa. It's a complete, high-protein meal that's perfect for dinner.

Nutritional Highlights:

- Chickpeas and tofu provide an excellent plant-based protein source, making this dish rich in protein and ideal for those looking to boost their plant-powered nutrition.

- Cauliflower offers fiber, antioxidants, and a low-calorie option that complements the richness of the tofu sauce.
- Saffron, though optional, adds a touch of luxury and enhances the flavor profile with its unique aroma.

This High-Protein Cauliflower and Chickpeas on Garlicky Whipped Tofu Sauce is a delicious, satisfying, and protein-packed dish that's as nutritious as it is flavorful!

Dinner 10: Tofu and Veggie Bites

Prep Time: 10 mins. Cooking Time: 20 mins

Ingredients:

- Broccoli, cut into florets
- Mushrooms, sliced
- Baby corn, blanched or boiled
- Cashews – 10-12, soaked
- Garlic – 4-5 cloves
- Ginger – 1-inch piece
- Tandoori masala – 1 tsp
- Chaat masala – 1 tsp

- Tofu – 1/2 block (cubed for blending)
- Vegan curd – 4 tbsp
- Roasted gram flour (besan) – 2 tbsp
- Chili flakes – 1 tsp
- Black pepper – 1/2 tsp
- Salt – to taste
- Mustard oil – 1 tsp

Method:

1. Blend the Paste:
   - In a blender, combine the soaked cashews, garlic, ginger, tofu, and vegan curd. Blend until smooth and creamy. There is no need to add water—the curd and tofu will provide enough moisture.
2. Prepare the Batter:
   - Transfer the blended mixture to a bowl. Add the roasted gram flour (besan), tandoori masala, chaat masala, chili flakes, black pepper, salt, and mustard oil. Stir well to form a thick batter.
3. Coat the Veggies:
   - Dip the blanched broccoli, mushrooms, and baby corn into the batter, ensuring they are fully coated.
4. Cook:
   - Air-fry: Preheat your air fryer to 180°C (350°F). Place the coated veggies in the air fryer basket in a single layer and cook for 10-12 minutes or until golden and crispy. You can lightly spray the veggies with oil if you prefer them extra crispy.
   - Alternatively, bake: Preheat your oven to 180°C (350°F). Place the coated veggies on a baking tray lined with parchment paper and bake for 12-15

minutes, flipping halfway through, until golden and crisp.

Serving Suggestion: Serve these protein-packed tofu and veggie bites as a snack, appetizer, or even a side dish with a tangy vegan dip or chutney. They're perfect for a light lunch or as part of a larger meal with a fresh salad! <u>Notes:</u>

- Cashews: Soaking cashews for a few hours will help create a smoother paste and enhance the creamy texture.
- Batter Consistency: If the batter feels too thick, you can add a little more vegan curd to adjust the consistency, but it should be thick enough to coat the vegetables.
- Tandoori Masala: Adds a smoky, flavorful kick, but feel free to adjust based on your preference for spice levels.

Green Salad for Tofu and Veggie Bites

<u>Ingredients:</u>

- Lettuce – 2 cups (any variety like romaine, iceberg, or butter lettuce)

- Cucumber – 1, thinly sliced
- Tomato – 1, diced
- Red onion – 1/4, thinly sliced
- Bell pepper – 1/2, thinly sliced (use red, yellow, or orange for a pop of color)
- Fresh coriander leaves – 1/4 cup, chopped
- Lemon juice – 1 tbsp
- Olive oil – 1 tbsp
- Salt – to taste
- Black pepper – a pinch
- Chili powder or sweet paprika (optional) – a pinch for extra zing
- Honey – 1 tsp (for a touch of sweetness)

Method:

1. Prepare the Salad:
- In a large mixing bowl, combine the lettuce, cucumber, tomato, red onion, bell pepper, and fresh coriander.

2. Dress the Salad:
- In a small bowl, whisk together the lemon juice, olive oil, salt, black pepper, and optional chili powder or sweet paprika. Add the honey to balance out the tang and provide a touch of sweetness. Taste and adjust the seasoning as needed.

3. Toss the Salad:
- Pour the dressing over the prepared salad and toss gently to combine, ensuring the veggies are evenly coated with the dressing.

Serving Suggestion: Serve this vibrant green salad alongside your Tofu and Veggie Bites for a light yet satisfying meal. The crisp vegetables, fresh herbs, and slightly sweet-spicy dressing pair wonderfully with the rich, spiced tofu and veggie bites. Notes:

- Extra Crunch: Add a handful of sunflower seeds, pumpkin seeds, or croutons for an added crunch.
- Other Veggies: You can also add other veggies like avocado, carrot ribbons, or radishes for extra texture and color.
- Creamy Dressing: If you prefer a creamier dressing, try mixing in a tablespoon of vegan yogurt or avocado for extra richness.

This salad is packed with vitamins, fiber, and antioxidants, making it the perfect complement to your high-protein tofu dish! Enjoy!

Chapter 4: Vegan Snacks1: Vegan Hot Chocolate

Prep Time: 5 mins Cooking Time:5 mins

<u>Ingredients:</u>

- 1 cup soy milk (or your preferred plant-based milk)
- 1/2 tsp Dutch cinnamon
- Pinch of pepper
- Pinch of nutmeg
- 2 tbsp raw cocoa powder (unsweetened)
- 2-3 dates or 1-2 tbsp maple syrup (for sweetness)
- 1/2 tsp turmeric powder (for added health benefits and color)
- 1/2 tsp vanilla extract
- Soy milk froth (for topping)

<u>Method:</u>

1. Blend the Ingredients:

- In a blender, combine the soy milk, Dutch cinnamon, pepper,nutmeg, raw cocoa powder, dates or maple syrup, turmeric powder, and vanilla extract. Blend well until everything is smooth and well combined.

2. Cook the Mixture:

- Pour the blended mixture into a saucepan. Heat over medium-low heat, stirring continuously to prevent burning or sticking. Stir gently until the hot chocolate is warmed through and reaches your desired temperature.

3. Froth the Soy Milk:

- While the hot chocolate is heating, use a milk frother to froth some soy milk. If you don't have a frother, you can also warm some soy milk in a separate saucepan and whisk vigorously until it becomes frothy.

4. Assemble:

- Once your hot chocolate is ready, pour it into a cup. Top it with the frothy soy milk for a creamy finish.

5. Optional Garnishes:

- For an extra touch, you can sprinkle a little more cinnamon or a pinch of cocoa powder on top.

Spiced vegan hot chocolate, with its blend of turmeric, cinnamon, and black pepper, offers more than just comfort. It provides numerous health benefits, from supporting immune function and digestion to boosting mood, promoting brain health, and managing weight. This delicious drink is a nourishing, guilt-free way to indulge while reaping the rewards of its potent, plant-based ingredients.

Vegan snack 2: Spicy & Tangy Soya Chunks Snack Ingredients:

Prep Time: 5 to 10mins Cooking Time:10 mins

- 1 cup dried soya chunks
- 1 tsp fennel seeds
- 1 onion, finely chopped
- 1 tomato, finely chopped
- 1 jalapeno, sliced (adjust according to spice preference)
- 1 tsp ginger-garlic paste
- 1/2 tsp salt (or to taste)
- 1 tsp chili powder
- 1 tsp gram masala (or garam masala)
- 1/2 tsp coriander powder
- 1-2 tbsp tomato ketchup (for sweetness)
- 1-2 tbsp soy sauce (for depth of flavor)
- Grated carrot (for garnish)
- Raw onion slices (for garnish)
- Fresh coriander leaves (for garnish)

<u>Method:</u>

1. Prepare the Soya Chunks:

- In a pot, boil enough water to cover the dried soya chunks. Once the water comes to a boil, add the soya chunks and let them cook for about 15 minutes.
- After 15 minutes, turn off the heat and let the soya chunks sit for another 5 minutes to soften.
- Drain the water and set the soya chunks aside to cool. Once cooled, squeeze out any excess water from the chunks.

2. Cook the Masala:
   - Heat a pan on medium heat. Add the fennel seeds and dry roast them for a minute to release their aroma.
   - Add the chopped onion and sauté until golden and soft. Then, add the chopped tomato, sliced jalapeno, and ginger-garlic paste. Cook for 2-3 minutes until the tomato softens and the mixture becomes aromatic.

3. Spice it Up:
   - Add the salt, chili powder, gram masala, and coriander powder to the pan. Stir well to combine all the spices and cook for another minute, allowing the flavors to meld together.

4. Add the Soya Chunks:
   - Add the soya chunks to the pan, tossing them to coat with the spices and masala. Stir in tomato ketchup and soy sauce for a tangy, slightly sweet, and savory flavor profile. Mix everything well and cook for another 3-4 minutes, allowing the soya chunks to absorb the flavors.

5. Garnish and Serve:
   - Once cooked, transfer the soya chunks to a serving plate.

- ○ Garnish with grated carrot, raw onion slices, and fresh coriander leaves for a fresh crunch and added flavor.

6. Enjoy:
   - ○ Serve this spicy, tangy, and high-protein soya chunks snack as a perfect midday snack, appetizer, or even a protein-packed topping for salads!

Spicy & Tangy Soya Chunks Snack is a powerhouse of nutrients and health benefits. Packed with high-quality plant-based protein, fiber, antioxidants, and anti-inflammatory spices, it supports a healthy digestive system, heart health, immunity, and weight management. This savoury snack is not only delicious but also nourishing for your body, providing energy, better digestion, and a balanced mood. Enjoy it as a healthy snack or appetizer with the added benefits of keeping you full and satisfied.

Snack 3: Vegan Energy Balls

Prep Time: 5 mins Cooking Time: 10mins
<u>Ingredients:</u>

- 1 cup roasted nuts (e.g., almonds, cashews, walnuts, or your choice)
- 1 cup roasted mixed seeds (pumpkin seeds, chia seeds, flax seeds, sunflower seeds, sesame seeds)
- 1 cup dates (pitted)
- A pinch of salt
- A pinch of cinnamon (optional)

<u>Method:</u>

1. Grind the Nuts and Seeds:
   - In a food processor, pulse the roasted nuts and mixed seeds together with a pinch of salt and cinnamon (if using).
   - Grind until you get a coarse mixture (you can leave a little texture for a crunchier bite).
2. Add the Dates:
   - Add the pitted dates to the mixture in the food processor and continue to blend until everything comes together and forms a sticky dough.
3. Form the Balls:
   - Once the mixture is well combined, use your hands to roll it into small balls (about 1-1.5 inch size).
   - If the mixture is too dry to form balls, you can add a small splash of water or a little extra date paste.
4. Chill (Optional):
   - For an extra firm texture, refrigerate the energy balls for about 30 minutes before serving.

These Vegan Protein Balls with Roasted Nuts and Seeds are a nutritional powerhouse, packed with plant-based protein, healthy fats, fiber, and antioxidants. They provide a wide range of health benefits, from boosting heart health and brain function to improving digestion and supporting muscle recovery. Whether you're fueling a workout, curbing hunger, or simply enjoying a nutritious snack, these protein balls are a delicious and wholesome option for anyone looking to nourish their body.

Vegan snack 4: Peanut Candy

Prep Time: 5 mins Cooking Time:5 mins Rest Time: 15 mins

<u>Ingredients:</u>

- 1 cup coconut sugar
- 1/2 tsp cardamom powder
- A pinch of salt
- 1 cup roasted peanuts
- Vegan butter or ghee (for greasing the plate)

<u>Method:</u>

1. Prepare the Sugar Mixture:

- In a pan, heat the coconut sugar over medium heat. Stir occasionally until it melts and thickens, forming a sticky syrup.
- Add the cardamom powder and a pinch of salt, and mix well. Continue cooking for another 1-2 minutes.

2. Add the Peanuts:
   - Once the sugar mixture has thickened, add the roasted peanuts. Stir well to coat the peanuts evenly with the sugar syrup.
   - Taste the mixture and adjust the sweetness if necessary, adding a little more coconut sugar if you prefer it sweeter.

3. Set the Candy:
   - Grease a plate or tray with vegan butter or ghee to prevent sticking.
   - Transfer the peanut mixture onto the plate and spread it evenly. Use the back of a spoon to press it down firmly.

4. Cool and Cut:
   - Allow the peanut candy to cool at room temperature for about 15-20 minutes. It will harden as it cools.
   - Once cooled, cut the candy into square or rectangular pieces.

Peanut candy, while a delicious treat, can offer various health benefits when eaten in moderation. It's a good source of protein, healthy fats, fiber, and antioxidants, making it a satisfying and nutrient-dense snack. The vitamins and minerals found in peanuts can improve heart health, boost brain function, support digestion, and promote healthy skin. However, due to the sugar content in many peanut candy recipes, it's best to enjoy this snack in moderation to avoid excessive calorie intake.

Vegan 5: Vegan Butter Cookies

Prep Time: 5 mins Cooking Time:10 to 12 mins

<u>Ingredients:</u>

- 1 cup almond flour
- 4 tbsp vegan butter
- 4 tbsp coconut sugar
- A pinch of salt
- 1 tsp vanilla extract
- Roasted almonds (for topping) <u>Method:</u>

1. Prepare the Cookie Dough:
   - In a mixing bowl, combine the almond flour, vegan butter, coconut sugar, a pinch of salt, and vanilla extract.

- ○ Mix everything well until it forms a dough. If the dough feels too dry, you can add a 2 teaspoon of water to bring it together.

2. Preheat the Oven:
   - ○ Preheat the oven to 220°C (428°F) for 10 minutes.

3. Shape the Cookies:
   - ○ Take small portions of dough and roll them into balls. Then gently flatten them into cookie shapes on a baking tray lined with parchment paper.
   - ○ Press a roasted almond gently in the center of each cookie.

4. Bake the Cookies:
   - ○ Place the tray in the preheated oven and bake at 180°C (350°F) for 10 to 12 minutes or until the edges of the cookies start to turn golden brown.

5. Cool and Serve:
   - ○ Remove the cookies from the oven and let them cool on the baking tray for about 5 minutes before transferring them to a wire rack to cool completely (about 1 hour for the best crisp texture).

These almond flour-based vegan butter cookies are crisp, delicious, and perfect for a light snack or dessert. Enjoy them with a cup of tea or coffee! Vegan butter cookies made with almond flour, coconut sugar, and vegan butter are a delightful and healthier alternative to traditional cookies. They offer protein, fiber, healthy fats, and a host of micronutrients, making them a more nutritious option when you're craving something sweet. With the added benefits of being dairy-free, lower glycaemic, and rich in antioxidants, these cookies can be enjoyed

as part of a balanced, health-conscious diet

Snack 6: Mixed Sprouts Salad

Prep Time: 10 mins

Ingredients:

- 1 cup mixed sprouts (mung beans, chickpeas, etc.)
- 1/2 cucumber, chopped
- 1 small onion, chopped
- 1 small tomato, chopped
- 1/4 cup pomegranate seeds
- 1 grated carrot
- 1/4 cup raw mango, chopped (optional for a tangy twist)
- Fresh coriander leaves, chopped
- Juice of 1 lime
- 1 tsp honey (optional for a touch of sweetness)
- Salt to taste
- 1 tbsp olive oil (optional)

Method:

1. Steam the Sprouts:

- ○ Steam the mixed sprouts for 5 minutes to soften them slightly while keeping their crunch. You can steam them in a steamer or microwave with a damp cloth for a few minutes.

2. Prepare the Salad:
    - ○ In a large mixing bowl, combine the steamed sprouts with the chopped cucumber, grated carrot, onion, tomato, pomegranate, raw mango (if using), and coriander leaves.

3. Dress the Salad:
    - ○ Squeeze the juice of a lime over the salad, drizzle with honey (if using), and season with salt to taste. Add olive oil for extra richness, if desired.

4. Toss and Serve:
    - ○ Mix everything together well to combine all the ingredients and flavors.

Serving Suggestion: This mixed sprouts salad is a refreshing and nutritious high-protein, high-fiber snack or side dish. The tangy raw mango and sweet pomegranate add a delightful balance to the crunchy sprouts and veggies! It's a fantastic choice for anyone looking to improve digestion, boost immunity, support heart health, and enjoy a tasty, hydrating, and low-calorie meal. Whether as a light meal or a refreshing side dish, this salad is sure to nourish both your body and taste buds!

Snack 7: High Protein & High Fiber Smoothie

Prep Time: 5-7 mins

This smoothie is packed with healthy fats, protein, and fiber from avocado, nuts, seeds, and coconut milk. It's perfect for a filling breakfast or a nutrient-dense snack. <u>Ingredients:</u>

- 1 ripe avocado (for healthy fats and creaminess)
- 1 cup fresh homemade coconut milk or soy milk (or storebought)
- 5 almonds (rich in protein and healthy fats)
- 2 walnuts (packed with omega-3s)
- 1 cashew (for creaminess)
- 3 pistachios (rich in protein and fiber)
- 1 tbsp mixed seeds (pumpkin seeds, sunflower seeds, flax seeds, chia seeds – for fiber and additional protein)
- 1 tbsp maple syrup (optional, for sweetness)
- A pinch of salt (optional, to enhance the flavors)
- Ice cubes (optional, for a colder smoothie)

<u>Method:</u>

1. Prepare the Ingredients:
   - If you're using homemade coconut milk or soy milk, make sure it's smooth and well-mixed.
   - If you'd like your smoothie to be colder, consider using frozen avocado or adding ice cubes.
2. Blend the Smoothie:
   - Add the avocado, coconut milk or soy milk, almonds, walnuts, cashews, pistachios, mixed seeds, and maple syrup into a blender.
   - Blend on high until smooth and creamy. If it's too thick, add a bit more coconut milk or water to achieve your desired consistency.
3. Taste and Adjust:
   - Taste the smoothie, and if you want it sweeter, add a little more maple syrup.
   - Optionally, add a pinch of salt to balance out the sweetness and bring out the flavors.
4. Serve:
   - Pour the smoothie into a glass and enjoy immediately.

Benefits:

- High Protein: From the nuts, seeds, and coconut milk.
- High Fiber: Avocado, nuts, and seeds provide excellent fiber, which supports digestion and keeps you full.
- Healthy Fats: Avocado, nuts, and seeds provide good fats that help with brain function and heart health.

Enjoy your creamy, nutritious, and satisfying high-protein, high-fiber smoothie!

Snack 8: Protein-Packed Gram Flour Cookies

Prep Time: 5 mins

Cooking Time: 8 to 10 mins

These protein-packed cookies are a perfect snack for when you're craving something sweet, filling, and nutritious. The combination of roasted gram flour, peanut butter, and nuts gives these cookies a boost of protein and healthy fats, while the natural sweeteners keep them wholesome and satisfying. <u>Ingredients:</u>

- 1 cup roasted gram flour
- 1/4 cup unsweetened crunchy peanut butter
- 2 tbsp jaggery or coconut sugar
- 2-3 tbsp skimmed milk (adjust as needed)
- 2 tbsp chopped nuts (almonds, pistachios, cashews)
- 1 tsp cardamom powder
- 1/2 tsp cinnamon powder
- Pinch of salt
- 1/4 tsp baking soda
- 1/4 tsp baking powder

<u>Method:</u>

1. Mix Dry Ingredients:
   - In a large bowl, combine roasted gram flour, cardamom powder, cinnamon powder, salt, baking soda, and baking powder.

2. Add Wet Ingredients:
   - Add peanut butter, jaggery (or coconut sugar), and mix everything together.
   - Gradually add skimmed milk, little by little, and knead the mixture into a soft dough.

3. Add Nuts:
   - Stir in the chopped almonds, pistachios, and cashews to add texture and crunch.

4. Shape the Dough:
   - Rest the dough for 10 minutes.
   - Shape the dough into small cookie-sized balls and gently flatten them with your fingers.

5. Bake the Cookies:
   - Preheat the oven to 180°C (350°F).
   - Place the cookies on a parchment-lined baking sheet, spaced apart.
   - Bake for 8 minutes at 180°C (350°F). Then, flip the cookies and bake for another 8 minutes.

6. Cool Down:
   - Once baked, let the cookies cool down for about 30 minutes on a cooling rack. This will help them firm up and enhance their flavor.

Serving Suggestions: These cookies are perfect as a mid-day snack, post-workout treat, or a quick breakfast with a cup of tea or coffee. Notes:

- Sweeteners: Adjust the level of sweetness by adding more or

  less jaggery/coconut sugar depending on your taste.
- Nuts: Feel free to swap the almonds, pistachios, or cashews with your favorite nuts or seeds.
- Texture: If you prefer a softer cookie, add a bit more milk. For crunchier cookies, bake them a bit longer.

These cookies are packed with protein, fiber, and healthy fats, making them the perfect guilt-free snack! Enjoy.

Snack 9: Lemon Blueberry Cake (Vegan & Healthy)

Prep Time: 5 mins

Cooking Time: 25 to 30 mins

This Lemon Blueberry Cake is a vibrant, light, and nourishing treat made with whole foods like oats, flaxseed, and fresh fruit. It's the perfect combination of tangy lemon, sweet blueberries, and a touch of honey for natural sweetness. It's vegan, gluten-free (when using gluten-free oats), and packed with nutrients! <u>Ingredients:</u>

- 1 ripe banana, mashed
- 1 tbsp flaxseed powder (mixed with 2 tbsp water to make a flax egg)
- Zest of 1 lemon
- 3 tbsp lemon juice
- 4 tbsp honey (or maple syrup for a vegan option)
- 2 tbsp vegan butter (or oil)
- 1 tsp baking powder
- 1/2 cup fresh blueberries
- 1 cup oats (use gluten-free oats if needed)
- 1/2 cup wholewheat flour (or oat flour for a gluten-free

option)
- 1/2 cup dairy-free milk (almond, soy, or oat milk)

Method:

1. Prepare the Pan:
    - Grease a cast-iron pan or any cake pan with a little bit of vegan butter or oil.
2. Mix Wet Ingredients:
    - In a large bowl, mash the banana until smooth.
    - Add the flaxseed powder (flax egg), dairy-free milk, vegan butter or oil, lemon zest, lemon juice, and honey.
    - Mix everything well until combined.
3. Add Dry Ingredients:
    - In the same bowl, add the baking powder, oats, and wholewheat flour.
    - Stir until fully combined.
4. Prepare Blueberries:
    - Toss the blueberries with 1 tablespoon of wholewheat flour (this will prevent the blueberries from sinking to the bottom of the cake).
    - Gently fold the blueberries into the batter.
5. Rest the Batter:
    - Let the batter rest for 15 minutes. This allows the oats to soak up some liquid, making the texture lighter and fluffier.
6. Bake the Cake:
    - Preheat the oven to 200°C (400°F).
    - Transfer the batter to the prepared pan and spread it out evenly.

- ○ Bake for 25-30 minutes or until a toothpick inserted into the center comes out clean.
7. Optional Topping:
   - ○ Once baked, you can sprinkle a bit of sugar on top for a light glaze.

Serving Suggestions:

- Serve warm with a cup of tea or coffee as a delicious afternoon snack.
- You can also top with fresh berries, a dollop of vegan yogurt, or a drizzle of maple syrup for extra sweetness.

<u>Notes:</u>

- Flax Egg: If you don't have flaxseed powder, substitute it with a regular egg if you prefer not to keep it vegan.
- Blueberries: Fresh or frozen blueberries work great. Just make sure to toss them in flour to prevent them from sinking during baking.

This Lemon Blueberry Cake is the perfect balance of sweet and tangy, with a light and moist texture. Enjoy a slice that's both nutritious and delicious!

This Vegan Lemon Blueberry Cake with flaxseed is not only a delightful treat but also a powerhouse of health benefits. Packed with omega-3 fatty acids, antioxidants, fiber, and vitamin C, this cake supports heart health, boosts immunity, aids digestion, and promotes healthy skin. Whether you enjoy it as a dessert, snack, or breakfast treat, it's a wholesome and delicious way to indulge without compromising on your health.

Vegan Snack 10: Chia Seed Pudding with Mixed Fruits and Nuts

Prep Time: 5 mins
Rest Time: 1 hour or overnight
Ingredients:

- 2-3 teaspoons chia seeds
- Water (enough to soak the chia seeds)
- 5 saffron strands
- 2 tablespoons chia seeds (for the pudding)
- 1 cup coconut milk (or any plant-based milk)
- A handful of almonds, cashews, pistachios, and walnuts, finely chopped
- 1 tablespoon mixed seeds (e.g., pumpkin, sunflower, flax seeds)
- 1 banana, chopped
- 1/2 mango, chopped (or any fruit of your choice)
- A handful of blueberries (or other berries)
- 1 tablespoon coconut sugar or honey (optional, depending on your sweetness preference)

<u>Method:</u>

1. Soak the Chia Seeds:
   - In a small bowl, add 2-3 teaspoons of chia seeds with water. Add the saffron strands and soak for about 2 hours (or refrigerate overnight for best results). This will allow the chia seeds to expand and absorb the water, creating a gel-like consistency.
2. Prepare the Pudding:
   - In a separate bowl, combine 2 tablespoons of chia seeds with 1 cup of coconut milk.
   - Add the finely chopped almonds, cashews, pistachios, and walnuts. Stir well to combine.
   - Add the mixed seeds, chopped banana, mango, and blueberries (or any fruit of your choice).
   - Sweeten with 1 tablespoon of coconut sugar or honey, if desired, and mix everything together.
3. <u>Chill and Serve:</u>
   - After mixing the pudding, let it sit in the fridge for at least 2 hours or overnight to thicken up.
   - Once ready to serve, top with more fresh fruit and nuts, if desired.

Benefits: This chia seed pudding is a nutrient-packed, delicious, and filling breakfast or snack. The combination of chia seeds, coconut milk, and mixed fruits provides healthy fats, fiber, and antioxidants, while the nuts add protein and crunch. Chia Seed Pudding with Mixed Fruits and Nuts supports heart health, digestion, and overall wellness.

It's a guilt-free treat that's perfect for any time of day.

Enjoy!

Conclusion:

As we conclude this culinary journey, my hope is that you feel inspired and empowered to embrace a healthier lifestyle with high-protein, high-fiber meals that seamlessly integrate into your daily routine. The recipes in this book are designed not only to nourish your body but also to elevate your overall well-being, enhance your fitness levels, and support your weight management and muscle-building goals. Best of all, these vibrant, flavorful dishes can be prepared in just 30 minutes, proving that healthy eating can be both efficient and enjoyable.

This cookbook is built on the foundation that food should serve both as nourishment and delight. Indian vegan cuisine, with its wealth of plant-based ingredients, offers a treasure trove of high-protein, high-fiber staples such as lentils, chickpeas, tofu, quinoa, whole grains, vegetables, seeds, and nuts.

These wholesome ingredients are naturally rich in essential nutrients, making them ideal for improving digestion, supporting muscle growth, and maintaining a healthy weight. The simplicity, efficiency, and versatility of Indian vegan meals provide a sustainable approach to fueling your body while savoring every bite.

Rooted in the principles of balanced nutrition, Indian cuisine emphasizes the use of fresh, whole foods. These meals are not only delicious but also designed to keep you fuller for longer, reduce unhealthy cravings, improve gut health, and provide sustained energy throughout the day. By combining proteins, fiber, and healthy fats, these dishes support your goal of feeling energized, satisfied, and nourished.

The key to success lies in consistency and simplicity. By stocking your pantry with high-quality, plant-based staples, you can create an array of satisfying meals without the need for complicated preparation or long hours in the kitchen. The recipes in this book celebrate the vibrant flavors of Indian cuisine while showcasing how accessible and convenient healthy eating can be.

As you embark on your journey toward better health, I encourage you to embrace the wisdom and benefits of Indian veganism. This time-tested approach to eating prioritizes plant-based nourishment, promoting optimal digestion, a robust immune system, enhanced energy, and overall well-being. The focus on protein-rich legumes, fiber-dense grains, fresh vegetables, and healthy fats will not only help you maintain muscle mass but also support gut health and vitality.

Incorporating these meals into your routine doesn't require drastic changes. Small, impactful choices—like opting for whole grains over refined ones, incorporating lentils into your dishes, and filling your plate with fresh vegetables and fruits—can make a significant difference. By adopting this mindful approach to eating, you'll naturally feel better, achieve your health goals, and build a body that reflects the vibrancy of the food you consume.

Healthy eating doesn't have to be complicated. With the pantry essentials and 30-minute recipes shared in this book, you can effortlessly prepare meals that nourish both your body and soul. Whether your goal is to lose weight, build muscle, or simply feel your best, these dishes are designed to keep you on track while delivering exceptional flavor and nutrition.

Thank you for choosing to embark on this journey of Indian veganism. By incorporating high-protein, high-fiber meals into your diet, you are making a powerful commitment to your health and well-being. These recipes provide a simple, effective, and delicious way to fuel your body with the nutrients it needs to thrive. Here's to a vibrant, healthy, and balanced life—filled with every meal you prepare, every bite you savor, and every goal you achieve. A life of radiant health and boundless energy is just 30 minutes away!

Acknowledgments

First and foremost, I want to express my deepest gratitude to my family, whose unwavering support, love, and encouragement made this cookbook possible. Your belief in me has been the foundation of my journey, and I couldn't have done this without you.

To the countless individuals who inspired my passion for cooking and healthy living, thank you. From my rich Indian heritage to the vibrant global community of vegan enthusiasts, your influence has shaped the recipes in this book.

A heartfelt thanks to everyone who shared their honest feedback during the creation of this cookbook—your insights have been invaluable in refining these recipes into something truly special.

To my readers, thank you for choosing this book and for taking a step toward a healthier, plant-based lifestyle. You inspire me every day to continue creating and sharing recipes that nourish both the body and soul.

Lastly, I dedicate this cookbook to those who believe that cooking is more than a task—it's an act of love, creativity, and care. May these recipes bring joy to your kitchen and inspire you to embrace the power of plant-based living.

With gratitude,
Sandhiya Iyyappan

SANDHIYA IYYAPPAN

Author Biography

Sandhiya Iyyappan is the accomplished author of *Against All Odds* and *Her Kingdom and Her Creation*, a thriving entrepreneur, and a passionate advocate for healthy living. Combining her love for cooking with her dedication to promoting plant-based nutrition, Sandhiya masterfully weaves creative storytelling into her talent for crafting wholesome, flavourful recipes.

Her journey into vegan cooking began as a personal quest for vibrant health and mindful eating. Inspired by her rich Indian heritage, Sandhiya has created a collection of high-protein, fibre-packed dishes that celebrate the bold, authentic flavours of traditional Indian cuisine while meeting the needs of modern, health-conscious lifestyles.

When she's not experimenting in the kitchen, Sandhiya channels her entrepreneurial spirit to inspire others to unlock their full potential. Her cookbook, *Weight-Watchers Delight: Indian Vegan Recipes Packed with High Protein & High Fiber in 40 Minutes*, is a testament to her belief that healthy eating can be both nourishing and deeply satisfying.

Through her work, Sandhiya empowers readers to embrace a plant-based lifestyle that fuels the body and mind, while discovering the pure joy of cooking and savouring every meal.

* 9 7 9 8 8 9 9 6 1 2 2 2 0 *